# RS TO MADNE SS

## The Victims of the
## HOLOCAUST

# Ted Gottfried

### Illustrations by Stephen Alcorn

THE HOLOCAUST

Twenty-First Century Books

Brookfield, Connecticut

The publisher wishes to thank the Wiener Library for its generous picture contribution to this book.

Chapter opening illustrations and design by Stephen Alcorn © www.alcorngallery.com

Photographs courtesy of National Archives: p. 19; National Archives/USHMM Photo Archives: pp. 28, 80; Institute of Contemporary History and Wiener Library Limited: p. 41; Professor Leopold Pfefferberg-Page Collection/USHMM Photo Archives: p. 50; Hulton Getty/Liaison Agency: p. 61; Archiwum Dokumentocji Mechanizney/USHMM Photo Archives: p. 71; Corbis/Bettmann: p. 91; Sara Trozki Koper Collection/USHMM Photo Archives: p. 97; Lisa Berg/USHMM Photo Archives: p. 104. Map by Joe LeMonnier.

Library of Congress Cataloging-in-Publication Data
Gottfried, Ted.
Martyrs to madness: the victims of the Nazis / Ted Gottfried.
p. cm.
Includes bibliographical references (p. ) and index.
Summary: Discusses how the Nazis came to power in Germany and the systematic brutalization they perpetrated on such groups as the Jews, Gypsies, Catholics, homosexuals, and others.
ISBN 0-7613- 1715-5 (lib. bdg.)
1. Holocaust, Jewish (1939–1945)—Juvenile literature. 2. World War, 1939–1945—Atrocities—Juvenile literature.
3. Germany—History—1933–1945—Juvenile literature. [1. Holocaust, Jewish (1939-1945). 2. World War, 1939-1945—Atrocities. 3. Germany—History—1933–1945.]

D804.34.G67   2000                    940.53'18—dc21                    99-057587

Published by Twenty-First Century Books
A Division of The Millbrook Press, Inc.
2 Old New Milford Road
Brookfield, Connecticut 06804

*In memory of my father,*
*Harry Gottfried*
*—Peace and Love*

## ACKNOWLEDGMENTS

I am grateful to personnel of the Judaica Room of the New York Central Research Library, the Mid-Manhattan Library, the Jewish Museum in New York, and the United States Holocaust Memorial Museum in Washington, D.C., as well as those at the central branch of the Queensboro Public Library. Thanks are also due to my friend George Fried for help with research, my fellow writers Kathryn Paulsen and Janet Bode, and—with much love—the contribution of my wife, Harriet Gottfried, who—as always—read and critiqued each chapter of this book as it was written.

All contributed, but any shortcomings in the work are mine alone.

—Ted Gottfried

# CONTENTS

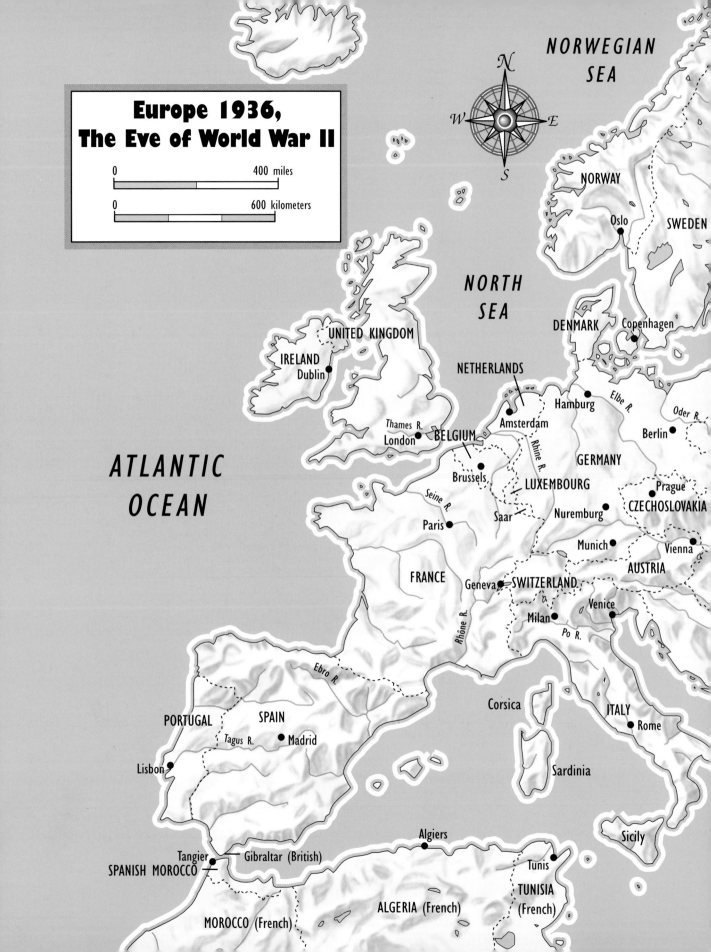

# Europe 1936, The Eve of World War II

0             400 miles

0             600 kilometers

NORWEGIAN SEA

NORWAY

SWEDEN

Oslo

NORTH SEA

DENMARK

Copenhagen

UNITED KINGDOM

IRELAND

Dublin

NETHERLANDS

Hamburg

Elbe R.

Oder R.

Amsterdam

Berlin

Thames R.

London

BELGIUM

Rhine R.

GERMANY

ATLANTIC OCEAN

Brussels

LUXEMBOURG

Prague

Seine R.

Saar

Nuremburg

CZECHOSLOVAKIA

Paris

Munich

Vienna

FRANCE

Geneva

SWITZERLAND

AUSTRIA

Venice

Rhône R.

Milan

Po R.

Ebro R.

Corsica

ITALY

PORTUGAL

SPAIN

Rome

Tagus R.

Madrid

Sardinia

Lisbon

Sicily

Algiers

Tangier

Gibraltar (British)

Tunis

SPANISH MOROCCO

TUNISIA (French)

ALGERIA (French)

MOROCCO (French)

# The Making of the Holocaust

**1**

*In Germany they came first for the Communists, and I didn't speak up because I wasn't a Communist. Then they came for the Jews, and I didn't speak up because I wasn't a Jew. They came for the trade unionists, and I didn't speak up because I wasn't a trade unionist. Then they came for the Catholics, and I didn't speak up because I was a Protestant. Then they came for me, and by that time no one was left to speak up.*[1]

Dr. Martin Niemöller

ar is killing. Regardless of a war's causes and long-term goals, the day-to-day aim of those who fight a war is to kill the enemy. The weapons are many, and they may change and improve over time, but their purpose remains the same: to kill.

But at what point in war does killing become murder? At what point does murder become slaughter? At what point does slaughter become *genocide*—the mass killing of whole groups of people because of their religion, their nationality, or the color of their skin? At what point does genocide become a holocaust?

*Holocaust* is the word used to describe the Nazi slaughter of two-thirds of the Jews in Europe before and during World War II. One out of every three Jews in the world was killed. Six million Jewish civilians—not soldiers—were murdered.

## The Untermenschen

They were killed because they were considered *Untermenschen*—the German word for people who are less than human. They were not alone. The Nazis considered many other groups—Slavs, Poles, Gypsies, all nonwhites, even Germans if they were homosexuals, Communists, disabled, or incurably ill—to be *Untermenschen*. They, too, were killed.

Some were prisoners of war. Some were civilians in occupied territories. Some were slave laborers in factories far from their homes. Some were patients in hospitals or asylums. Like the Jews, they were murdered in a variety of ways.

Untold millions: the very old and the very young; women as well as men; nobody knows exactly how many. They didn't fight in the war; they weren't accidental civilian casualties; they were deliberately tortured, killed, starved to death, allowed to die for lack of medical treatment or from exposure. They were the victims of "crimes against humanity," according to the judgment of international law, and of the civilized nations of the world.[2]

International law says that a nation may not murder its own citizens. The law says that minorities within a country may not be persecuted. Robbery, rape, and murder of civilians in occupied territories is forbidden. Slave labor is prohibited.

The rules of war say that "belligerents must treat prisoners humanely."[3] They provide that "military wounded and sick must be cared for."[4] The taking of hostages, reprisals, and torture are forbidden.

The Nazis broke all of these laws and others.

## What Do You See?

How could they do such things?

They could do them because humanity is in the eye of the beholder. The butchery begins with the clouding of that eye. It starts with what that eye sees when it looks at another person.

If it sees less than a human being, then there is reason for a sense of superiority, for contempt, for hatred, and for fear. If those it sees are regarded as less than human—*Untermenschen*—then the rules of how to treat one's fellow man or woman do not apply. If people are seen as not only different but evil because they think differently, dress differently, believe differently, or look different, then they are a threat that has to be dealt with before it is too late.

Fear is one of the driving forces of prejudice. It breeds hatred. It fuels violence. Once that violence is unleashed, it must run its course.

That is the horrible lesson of the Holocaust. The violence forever seeks new victims. Jews, Gypsies, Slavs, Serbs, Greeks, gays, Catholics, nonwhites, prisoners of war—it devours everything different, everything in its path until, in the end, it devours itself.

And it begins always with denying the other person's humanity.

# 2

# The First To Fall

World War I ended in November 1918. Germany was defeated. Years of turmoil followed.

There was not enough food and people starved. There was no work. Money was worthless; the German mark was "worth less than a quarter trillionth of a dollar."[1] The people were miserable, and they were bitter.

Germany's first democratic government was formed after the war. However, that government, the Weimar Republic, was weak and seemed unable to relieve the people's suffering. It came under constant attack from the extreme left and the extreme right. This was the soil in which the seeds of the Holocaust were planted.

## The Spartacists

People who are defeated and hungry and jobless become bitter and frustrated. They gather in groups, small and large, and together they seek the cause of their misery. They want to know who is responsible; they need to find someone to blame.

In post–World War I Germany, people belonging to the political left blamed the business people and manufacturers who made money from the war. They blamed the police and the army for putting down strikes by working people.

They blamed Germany's postwar Weimar Republic for having set itself up in place of a genuine Communist revolution like the one that had recently taken place in Russia.

Groups on the left ranged from middle-of-the-road Socialists and trade unionists to dedicated Communists. In general they wanted government social-welfare programs, benefits for labor and the organization of workers into labor unions, a redistribution of wealth from the rich to the poor, and the national-ization of banks and major industries such as coal, steel, electric power, and transportation. The most militant of these groups were the Spartacists. They wanted to overthrow the government by violence, and they brought that vio-lence to the streets of cities throughout Germany.

## Nazi Storm Troopers

The left-wing groups were met by violence from the right. The Nazis were only one of many right-wing groups at the time. Most of them wanted Germany to violate the Treaty of Versailles (which called for Germany to disarm and to pay reparations to the Allies), to outlaw labor unions, to jail all Communists and Socialists, and to confiscate the property of Jews. They wanted a strong central government like the one under the kaiser, before the war. One-man rule had marked the kaiser's reign, the opposite of the Weimar government, in which people elected officials to represent their interests.

In March 1920, a right-wing movement tried to overthrow the government. Street battles were fought with trade unionists. In the end, the government was saved by a general strike of workers who preferred the weak Weimar democ-racy to strict rule by the antilabor right.

Of the many different groups on the right, the most extreme were the German Racist Freedom party in the north of Germany, and the National Socialist German Workers' party (the Nazis) in Munich. These groups demanded the overthrow of the republic. They demanded the punishment of politicians who, they claimed, had sold Germany out to the victors at the end of the war. They were against Communists and trade unionists. They believed in an extreme form of patriotism based on the superiority of the German people and love of the German Fatherland.

The Nazis organized ex-soldiers into bands of storm troopers—uniformed gangs of street bullies—to put muscle into their cause. These storm troopers fought violent street battles with Communists and trade unionists. Left-wing party headquarters and newspaper offices were attacked, vandalized, and torched. People who got in the way of the storm troopers were bullied. There were beatings and killings.

Communists, leftists, trade unionists, and Social Democrats were the first victims of the Nazis.

## The Jewish Germans

Some of the victims were innocent bystanders. Others had been deliberately targeted—not because they were political opponents but rather because they were Jews. The Nazi party had singled them out.

In February 1920, the Nazis had issued a twenty-five-point party program. Point Four declared that "only those of German blood, whatever their creed, may be members of the nation. Accordingly no Jew may be a member of the nation."[2]

Jews, however, had been members of the German nation for hundreds of years. They had fought in Germany's wars. They were part of German culture and German life. They were Jews but considered themselves German as well. They had always known persecution: being barred from owning land, attending certain schools, and engaging in some trades. They had even been subjected to physical abuse, as had Jews in other countries. Still, this had not shattered their pride in being German.

Now, it seemed, they were to be German no longer.

**Nazi leader Adolf Hitler (giving the Nazi salute) at a party rally in Nuremberg, Germany, in 1928**

## Spreading the Poison

The anti-Semitism (hatred of Jews) that had existed for centuries merged with the violent and aggressive anti-Semitism of the Nazis and spread. More and more, ordinary Germans blamed the Jews for their country's defeat in World War I. It was said that Jewish manufacturers had overcharged the government for supplies and that Jewish bankers had charged too high an interest rate on government loans. Jews, it was muttered, were responsible for the inflation that was making German money worthless. The Jews were hoarding gold.

Very little of this was true, but much of it was believed.

The poison spread. Jews—both teachers and students—were excluded from some schools and universities. Some hospitals barred Jewish doctors from practicing in them. Professional organizations and clubs barred Jews from membership.

It got worse. Jewish shops were vandalized by Nazi storm troopers. Synagogues were defaced. Insults were hurled, and people were beaten simply because they were Jewish. Anti-Semitism became so widely accepted that it became dangerous to speak out against it.

Attitudes were described by German historian Franz Bohm in a lecture on anti-Semitism in the Weimar Republic: "For anti-Semitism hundreds of thousands were ready to ascend the barricades," he summed up. "Against anti-Semitism hardly a hand stirred."[3]

The Nazis had achieved their goal of stirring up hatred against the Jews and convincing a majority of the German people that the Jews were responsible for all the county's ills. They had persuaded the Germans that Jews were not like other Germans. Jews were different. They could be treated differently. They could be persecuted. They could be killed.

## Three Dead Policemen

So could other people perceived as a threat by the Nazis. Among those killed by the Nazis were three Munich policemen who died on November 9, 1923. They were the victims of what history has come to call the Beer Hall Putsch.

It began the night before. Some three thousand Munich businessmen were meeting in a local beer hall when armed storm troopers marched into the hall and announced that the Nazi revolution had begun. Another band of storm troopers had tried to seize the War Ministry but had failed and were surrounded by soldiers. When morning came, the Nazis in the beer hall set out to rescue them.

Police blocked their way. Shooting broke out. When it was over, many policemen had been wounded and three lay dead. Sixteen Nazis were also dead. The leader of the Nazis, however, had fled, unhurt.

His name was Adolf Hitler.

## Mein Kampf

Hitler was caught and tried for his role in the killing of the three policemen. He was sent to prison but remained there for only nine months. During that time he wrote *Mein Kampf* (*My Struggle*), a combination of personal history and Nazi propaganda that became a best-seller throughout Germany.

When discussing "the art of leadership" in *Mein Kampf*, Hitler stressed "concentrating the attention of the people on a single adversary, making different opponents appear as if they belonged to the same category."[4] The "single adversary" was what Hitler called the "Jewish world conspiracy."[5] According to Hitler, and despite centuries of evidence to the contrary, Jews did not work. They schemed to live off the work of others. Jews were "always a parasite," he wrote, "in the body of other peoples."[6] In this way he focused the discontent of the German people and assigned blame for their suffering to the Jews among them.

Assigning other opponents to the same category as the Jews required a system of logic peculiar to the Nazis. As a nation, except for the Jews, Germany was Christian—roughly two-thirds Protestant, one-third Catholic. Yet Hitler proclaimed himself "against Christianity itself."[7] He called practicing Christians in Germany "traitors to the people"[8] and declared that they "will have to be suppressed."[9]

Sometimes Nazi propaganda focused on Catholics. One example from the Nazi newspaper *Voelkischer Beobachter* (*Ethnic/Racial Observer*) shows how a particular foe could be redefined to fit the despised Jewish category. "The Pope," the hate sheet announced, "is a Jew whose real name is Lippmann."[10]

If Protestant Christians and the Catholic pope could be put in the same category as such despised enemies as Jews and Communists and trade unionists, then who could escape Nazi bigotry? Seemingly no one was secure. Yet there was one group the Nazis held above suspicion.

They were called Aryans.

# The Growing Hit List

3

itler and the Nazis took over the German government in 1933. The year before, Hitler had received 30.1 percent of the votes in an election for president of Germany. In a subsequent runoff election, he had received 36.8 percent of the votes cast. His popularity was such that on January 30, 1933, the man who had beaten him, President Paul von Hindenburg, was forced to appoint Hitler chancellor of Germany, a position that was actually more powerful than that of president. When Hindenburg died in August 1934, the two offices were merged and Hitler became dictator.

For more than a decade the Nazis had preached hatred. Now they did not hesitate to make their views official policy and to put them into action. At the core of these views was a theory of racial purity.

## Aryan Purity

The Nazis believed that the German people were Aryans—the descendants of a superior Indo-Iranian civilization, a warrior race that had swept across Europe in prehistoric times. They defined a member of this Aryan race as "a Caucasian of non-Jewish descent."[1] However, neither Slavs, nor Serbs, nor southern Europeans, nor Asians, nor Africans, nor many other non-Jews were considered Aryan by the Nazis. To be Aryan, you had to have German blood.

They said that blood was sacred. Its purity had to be guarded against intermarriage, hereditary diseases, mental illness, homosexual leanings, and moral weaknesses like alcoholism or promiscuity. Defects had to be searched out and prevented from spreading so that the strength and superiority of the Aryan master race would not be weakened.

This kind of thinking led to the Sterilization Law of July 1933. "The purity of the German blood is essential to the continued existence of the German people," proclaimed those who incorporated the act into the anti-Semitic Nuremberg Laws two years later.[2] By that time the sterilization program was in full swing.

## The Sterilization Program

*Sterilization* is a medical procedure that takes away a person's ability to conceive a child. It can be done with drugs or surgically. Sometimes, for a variety of reasons, people have themselves sterilized voluntarily. In Nazi Germany, some 400,000 people were sterilized by force.

Officially, the program was aimed at those with undesirable conditions that were considered hereditary—that might be passed on from parent to child. Courts were set up to determine which illnesses—mental and physical—were hereditary, and which patients should be forcibly sterilized. Doctors, psychologists, and drug companies were all part of the program.

Sometimes, the selection of persons for sterilization was influenced by politics. To the Nazis, Communists and trade unionists were insane. If they were crazy, then it was justifiable to prevent their madness from being passed on to future generations. Nobody knows how often opposition to Nazi policies was punished by forcible sterilization.

The techniques used for sterilization were highly experimental. Many of the victims reported side effects. A decrease in the desire to have sex was a common result. Mental stability was affected, particularly among patients suffering from schizophrenia, acute depression, and other illnesses of the mind. Some of those who were sterilized were unable to have sex again after the procedure. Alcoholism, epilepsy, and other physical conditions worsened. There were cases of suicide.

The program ended when World War II began. As it drew to a close, the Nazis considered a further use for it. Perhaps the "Slavic populations in German-occupied Europe could be brought to extinction by mass steriliza-tions."[3] Toward this end, experiments would later be done on Jews and Gypsies in the concentration camps, places of confinement and slave labor, which the Nazis set up for *Untermenschen* and political prisoners.

## Persecution of Catholics

When the sterilization program was begun in 1933, there were strong protests from the Catholic Church. The Nazis struck back by ordering the Catholic Youth League to disband. That was only the first step in the organized persecu-tion of German Catholics by the Nazis.

Throughout 1933 and 1934, "thousands of Catholic priests, nuns and lay leaders were arrested."[4] The charges against them ranged from "immorality" to "smuggling foreign currency."[5] Although there was little evidence against them, Nazi justice was swift and they were sent off to the newly constructed concen-tration camps.

Catholic newspapers and magazines were forbidden to publish. Gestapo (Nazi secret police) agents violated the confessional booths in Catholic churches. Storm troopers vandalized some churches. On June 30, 1934, the leader of Catholic Action, a social-justice wing of the church, was murdered.

## Legalizing Anti-Semitism

During this period, the Nazis' anti-Semitism was put into law. The Hitler administration decreed that Jews could not hold government jobs, teach or study in universities, or work in journalism, radio, the theater, or films. Then they were barred from Germany's stock exchanges. Finally, they were forbidden to practice law or medicine. The government put up billboards all over Germany urging the people not to buy from Jewish shopkeepers.

German trade unions also came under attack by the government. Storm troopers raided union offices, smashed property, and arrested union officials. Nazi administrators took over management of the unions.

Both the Communist party and the Social Democratic party, which had been elected to govern Germany before Hitler, were outlawed. Their members were rounded up on made-up charges. The roundups were marked by beatings and violence.

In March 1933, the first concentration camp was built in a town called Dachau, 10 miles (16 kilometers) outside of Munich in southern Germany, 30 miles (48 kilometers) north of the Alps. It was soon filled with 15,000 political prisoners who had been arrested in the east German state of Prussia. Wiping out political opposition was a priority of the Hitler government.

## The "Night of the Long Knives"

Heading the list of those to be wiped out were longtime members of the Nazi party whom Hitler saw as a threat to his control. Chief among them were Ernst Röhm, who had organized the Nazi street fighters in the early days; and Gregor Strasser, who had led the Nazi party while Hitler was in jail. Hitler believed they were plotting with former German chancellor Kurt von Schleicher to overthrow him.

In Berlin, on June 30, 1934, Gregor Strasser was seized by the Gestapo and killed. General von Schleicher and his wife were also murdered. Special police rounded up nearly eighty-five of Ernst Röhm's followers, stood them up against a Berlin wall, and executed them.

Röhm himself was vacationing at an inn not far from Munich when a party of armed men led by Adolf Hitler himself burst in on him. Two men with Röhm

Atrocities performed on Jews were merely rumors perpetuated by Jews themselves, Nazis claimed, and as retaliation German citizens were urged not to patronize Jewish businesses.

were immediately shot dead. Hitler arrested Röhm and ordered him to kill himself, but Röhm refused. Hitler then gave the order, and Röhm was executed on July 1.

Hitler justified the murder on the grounds that Röhm, who was a homosexual and had recruited his followers among homosexuals, was morally corrupt. Of course, Hitler had known this throughout the many years that he and Röhm had been allies. Nevertheless, he condemned Röhm as "a homosexual [who] will fill all positions of authority with other homosexuals."[6]

In the wake of the Röhm murder strong laws were passed against homosexuality. A special section was set up at Gestapo headquarters to deal with cases involving homosexuals. Increasingly harsh punishments were decreed for engaging in homosexual acts.

The murders of Röhm, Strasser, and their supporters would come to be known as the "Night of the Long Knives."[7] Hitler said that seventy-seven traitors had been executed. The actual number of Nazi victims of other Nazis that night is not known because of secret orders issued by Hermann Göring and Heinrich Himmler to destroy all records relating to the incident. As minister of the interior for the state of Prussia, Göring had created the *Geheime Staatspolizei* (Secret State Police) and appointed Himmler to run it. Himmler would expand the *Geheime Staatspolizei*, which became known to the world as the Gestapo.

## The Nuremberg Laws

As Hitler was tightening his grip on the nation, Nazi violence was spreading beyond Germany's borders. A strong Nazi movement was growing in Austria among those with German blood who considered themselves Aryans and wanted their country to become part of a greater Germany. They were opposed by the Austrian chancellor, Engelbert Dollfuss.

On July 25, less than a month after the Night of the Long Knives, Nazis burst into Dollfuss's office in Vienna and shot him. They barricaded themselves in the office for four hours, watching him bleed to death. He was one of the earliest Austrian victims of the Nazis. Many more would follow.

Austrian anti-Semitism was as strong as the German variety, but as yet without the force of law that was taking shape in Germany under the Nazis. On September 15, 1935, the so-called Nuremberg Laws went into effect in Germany. They said that while Jews remained "subjects" of Germany, they were no longer German citizens and had none of the rights and privileges of citizens.[8] They forbid both marriage and sex between Jews and Aryans. Jews were prohibited from employing female Aryan servants younger than age thirty-five.

The Nuremberg Laws were quickly amended by thirteen decrees meant to isolate Jews even more. If Jews left the country, they were forbidden to take more than a minimum amount of money and valuable property. German groceries, butcher shops, bakeries, and pharmacies, encouraged by the government, often refused to sell them food and medicine. "At least one half of them," according to historian William L. Shirer, "were without means of livelihood" after the Nuremberg Laws went into effect.[9]

## An Aryan Victim

Most of the Protestant and Catholic religious leaders of Germany did not protest the treatment of the Jews. However, 807 Protestant ministers and other church leaders were arrested for opposing the Nazis in 1937. Hundreds more were arrested in the years that followed.

The most famous religious leader to oppose the Nazis was Dr. Martin Niemöller. He had been a submarine commander in World War I and a strong opponent of the Weimar Republic. At first he had welcomed the Nazi regime, but he soon became appalled at its violent policies. He spoke out against it in his church. "No more are we ready to keep silent," he declared, "when God commands us to speak."[10]

On July 1, 1937, Niemöller was arrested. He was taken to prison in Berlin and held there for eight months before he was put on trial. He was convicted of "abuse of the pulpit," fined two thousand German marks, sentenced to the time he had already served, and released.[11]

As he left the courtroom, Niemöller was seized by the Gestapo. He was sent to the concentration camp at Sachsenhausen, and from there to Dachau. Miraculously, he survived seven years' of imprisonment in the camps and was liberated by Allied troops at the end of the war. He became a symbol of how a German Aryan, too, could suffer at the hands of the Nazis.

## Other Lands, Other Casualties

Aryans could be persecuted and non-Aryans could be allies when it suited Hitler's purposes. In *Mein Kampf* he had written that his goal of conquering Europe required at least one non-Aryan ally: Italy. Since the early 1920s, Italy had been ruled by the dictator Benito Mussolini. His strong-arm methods and rise to power had provided a road map for Hitler to follow.

In 1936, Italy attacked Ethiopia. Mussolini's air force dropped "canisters of mustard gas on civilians," a violation of international law. Red Cross units were also "decimated by the gas."[12] Despite the condemnation of the League of Nations and protests from outraged governments around the world, Italy conquered Ethiopia.

Hitler was unmoved by the bombing of helpless African civilians. On the contrary, he saw it as an opportunity to form the alliance he wanted with Mussolini. Germany and Italy signed a mutual-defense pact on November 1, 1936.

A half year later, it was the German air force—built up in violation of the treaty that ended World War I—that was bombing unarmed civilians in Guernica, Spain. At that time a civil war was raging in Spain between the armed forces of the elected republic and those of right-wing General Francisco Franco, who was trying to overthrow it. The Nazis sided with Franco.

"Hundreds of people . . . were killed by German warplanes which swept out of the skies . . . to strafe a marketplace and farm houses. . . . Junkers and Heikel bombers dropped half-ton bombs, grenades and firebombs and fired mercilessly at peasants working in the fields."[13] The event inspired Spanish artist Pablo Picasso to paint *Guernica*, a moving testament to the inhumanity of Nazi war making.

## The Nazis in Austria

There was little such violence when Germany took over Austria in March 1938. After German troops had crossed the border and Hitler had entered the capital city of Vienna at the head of forty tanks, however, the arrests of those opposed to the Nazis began. According to historian Alan Bullock, there were "76,000 in Vienna alone."[14] Among them was Austrian Chancellor Kurt von Schuschnigg. Seized by the Gestapo, he later joined Niemöller in the concentration camps of Sachsenhausen and Dachau.

The Nazis were already well established in Austria, and the takeover was approved by 99 percent of the voters in both Germany and Austria. The Austrians accepted Nazi anti-Semitic laws. "Immediately behind the German army came a large force of 40,000 police and SS Death's Head Formations who began the systematic persecution of Austria's 300,000 Jews," reports one historian.[15] The Reich Center for Jewish Emigration, which would later oversee the shipment of victims to the death camps, was set up in Vienna by Austrian-born Nazi Adolf Eichmann.

Crowds gathered in Vienna for "rubbing parties" in which uniformed Nazi bullies forced Jews to scrub the streets with their bare hands or with toothbrushes.[16] One such incident is described by an English journalist: "SA men (Nazi storm troopers) dragged an elderly Jewish worker and his wife through the applauding crowd. Tears ran down the cheeks of the old woman, and . . . I could see how the old man, whose arm she held, tried to stroke her hand. 'Work for the Jews, at last work for the Jews,' howled the crowd. 'We thank our Führer, he has made work for the Jews!'"[17]

## Kristallnacht

The fury of the German Nazis was more destructive than that of the Austrians. It was also more carefully arranged. On November 9, 1938, Nazi Minister of Propaganda Joseph Goebbels wrote an order that "spontaneous demonstrations" against Jews should be "organized and executed" that night. The result was *Kristallnacht*—the Night of Broken Glass.

Some 7,500 Jewish stores and businesses had their windows, doors, and showcases smashed by rampaging young Nazis. By morning, 800 Jewish establishments had been completely destroyed, with hundreds of millions of dollars in damage. Homes of Jewish families were also broken into, looted, and set afire. Some Jewish women were raped, and more than 90 Jews were killed. In addition, 191 synagogues were burned down. As the smoke was clearing, 30,000 Jews were rounded up for shipment to concentration camps.

## Murder Saves Money

With the country on the verge of war, most non-Nazi Germans did not pay much attention to what was happening with the Jews. German troops would soon be on the march, and patriotic fever was high. In this climate it was easy for Hitler to issue a secret order in the spring of 1939.

The directive kicked off the Euthanasia Program, authorizing the killing "of all mentally and physically handicapped children and adults" whose condition was judged incurable.[18] Later it was expanded to include old people who were hopelessly ill.

Asylums and nursing homes for the elderly were expensive to run. The Nazis decided it would be cheaper to kill those who could no longer take care of themselves. Savings over a 10-year period were projected at 885,439,800 reichsmarks for the 70,273 people who were put to death under the program. All were Aryan Germans. Jews and others were killed in Germany as the war began, but not in the Euthanasia Program.

The program's code name was *T4*. The first killings were of children, who were injected with a poisonous drug. Hitler himself ordered that the method be changed to death by carbon monoxide gas. To accomplish this, the first Nazi gas chamber was designed by an officer from the SS (Hitler's personal guard unit) and disguised as a shower room. After the killings, doctors signed false cause-of-death certificates that were sent to the victims' families along with an urn of ashes and a letter of condolence. The families were never told that their loved ones had been executed.

The program ended officially on September 1, 1941, due to fear of protests from the clergy and the public. Some of those who were dedicated to the program, however, continued the practice by allowing hopelessly ill patients—particularly children—to starve to death. Among the four hundred medical specialists who participated in *T4*, ninety-six were later transferred to the death camps. Here their expertise was applied to killing on the massive scale we have come to call the Holocaust.

**4**

**Legacy of Hate**

**H**atred of Jews was the basis of the Holocaust. But why were they hated? The answer is complicated. It reaches far back into European history.

The Jews were small in number. They were a minority religion in the Muslim world, in the Catholic world, and in the Protestant world. They lived among many other peoples, but would not merge with them. They would not compromise their religion or alter their code of behavior. They dressed differently, worshiped differently, and often spoke a different language. Throughout history, their separateness was resented.

## The Diaspora

Periodically, their refusal to give up their religion and convert became a life-and-death issue. Jews fled Spain and Portugal for Britain and France. They fled France for Italy, the Netherlands, and Belgium. They fled to the independent German states and to Austria and Hungary. Fleeing persecution, they migrated farther eastward, settling in Romania, Bulgaria, Poland, Latvia, Lithuania, Ukraine, and Russia.

They used a Greek word to describe the result of their wanderings: Diaspora. It means "scattering" or "to scatter about."[1] It describes the spread of groups of Jews throughout the world where they lived among different cultures and lifestyles.

When these small groups of Jews came to each new place, they were outsiders. The land was already owned. Jobs were already taken. Mostly, these people who dressed and believed differently were not welcomed. They were persecuted.

## Adapting to Circumstances

The persecution took similar forms in different parts of Europe. Jews were forced to live in ghettos. Curfews were imposed on them. They were forbidden to mix with Christians. They could not own land. They could not practice law or medicine. They were barred from certain schools. They had none of the rights of citizenship extended to others. They had to seek new ways to make a living, ways that would not threaten the non-Jews.

In much of eastern Europe, sewing was a craft open to Jews. Many of them became expert tailors. They were among the first to use the newly invented sewing machines. Many traveled from place to place with their sewing machines on their backs. They turned fabric into clothing, and in northern Europe they sewed pelts and became furriers.

Other Jews moved into exotic professions such as carving diamonds in Amsterdam and making gold and silver jewelry in Toledo, Spain. Jewish communities grew up around the craftspeople. They also grew up around those Jews who prospered through trade and money changing.

## The Money Changers

Driven from place to place through the centuries, the Jews had bartered in order to survive. They had traded what goods they had for what food they needed. Europe had been split up into many small states, each with its own money, and some Jews learned the relative value of these currencies. They became master traders and experts on the currencies of other countries.

In those times, bands of thieves preyed on the traveling merchants of the European states. An Amsterdam wine merchant carrying a large sum of money to Bordeaux to buy wine was easy prey for highwaymen. Even if he reached France without being robbed, he might be cheated in the exchange of Dutch guilders for French francs.

The Jewish money changer solved these problems. He took the Dutch guilders and in exchange gave the wine merchant a note to a Jewish money changer in Bordeaux who paid him back in francs. The note was in Hebrew and described the merchant so that there could be no mistakes. For this the money changer charged a small commission.

Sometimes the money changer helped out as a moneylender, who would arrange for a Jewish colleague in another city to provide a merchant with money to purchase goods. The merchant would repay the original moneylender after returning with the goods and selling them. Again, a small fee was charged. In this way, some Jews became involved in the banking system of Europe.

## Image of the Money-Grubber

Their knowledge of trade and currencies was very valuable to the merchants, the bankers, even the governments of the countries in which they settled. Jewish money changers were widely sought for their advice. Their activities stimulated trade.

Cities like Venice in Italy and others in France, Germany, and far-off Poland invited them to settle there in order to encourage commerce. These Jews became important to the economies of the countries in which they settled. Other Jews both profited and suffered by that success, however.

They profited because, where it was possible, the more successful Jews financed them in business ventures such as small shops or sewing factories. There was employment for other Jews in Jewish businesses. However, they suffered because Jewish success was envied by non-Jews who saw it as money-grubbing and who identified all Jews—even those who had very little—with the manipulation of money. To the peasant tilling the land, with no experience in trade or exchanging money, Jews were viewed as un-Christian and their handling of money as the work of the devil. Jews who had no more to do with banking than these peasants themselves were hated as money-grubbers—and persecuted.

## Rumors of Ritual Murder

Because the Jews had a different religion, horrible rumors sprang up regarding their rituals. In England it was believed that Jews kidnapped young boys, killed them, and used their blood to color the cakes used in their Passover ceremonies. Twenty Jews executed for one such crime were later found innocent.

Charges of ritual murder spread across Europe. They reached Poland and Russia and there were pogroms—frenzies of pillaging, rape, and murder—against Jewish communities. Finally such rumors died out, only to be replaced by an accusation that would be even more widely believed.

This accusation would be at the heart of the most anti-Semitic document ever circulated. It was called *The Protocols of the Learned Elders of Zion*.

## The Protocols

The *Protocols* first appeared in a newspaper of the Russian government in 1903 and later were distributed throughout Russia as part of a religious pamphlet by a government agent posing as a Russian Orthodox priest. They were presented as a report on a series of meetings supposedly held in Switzerland in 1897. In these meetings Jews were said to have made plans "to disrupt Christian civilization and erect a world state under their joint rule. Liberalism and socialism were to be the means of subverting Christendom; if subversion failed, all the capitals of Europe were to be sabotaged."[2]

In eastern Europe, particularly in those parts ruled by the Russian czar, the *Protocols* were used to redirect the mounting discontent of the serfs who worked on the large farmland estates owned by the aristocracy. These serfs were little better than slaves, and from the 1890s onward they posed an ongoing threat of revolution in Russia. The rulers used the *Protocols* to turn the serfs' fury away from themselves and toward the Jews.

The document was a forgery created by the Russian secret police. Nevertheless, it served its purpose. Most of the serfs couldn't read, but the *Protocols* were read to them. Old stories of ritual murders were revived, and a new wave of pogroms was deliberately provoked. These were so extensive as to cause a mass migration of Jews from Russia. The United States and other governments issued protests against the bloodshed to the czarist regime.

## The Spread of the Protocols

Past rumors of ritual murder had spread from west to east. Now translations of the *Protocols* spread from east to west and across the Atlantic as well. There was violence against Jews in Austria. In France a Jewish army officer named Alfred Dreyfus was charged with treason as a member of the *Protocols* conspiracy, and a wave of anti-Semitism swept over the country. In the United States, wealthy automobile manufacturer Henry Ford reprinted excerpts from the *Protocols* in his newspaper, the *Dearborn Independent*, and conducted a seven-year campaign to prove that Jewish Communists and Jewish international bankers were partners in the anti-Christian conspiracy.

In Germany in the early 1920s, Walther Rathenau, a Jew, was named foreign minister of the Weimar Republic. Two young Nazis who had read the *Protocols* and "believed that Rathenau had conspired with fellow Jews to dominate the world," sprayed him with machine-gun fire and blew up his car with a hand grenade.[3] They were part of a Nazi group calling itself the "Murder Exploding Detachment," which had targeted prominent Jews in Germany who were

The Protocols of the Learned Elders of Zion was an influential, far-reaching publication, as demonstrated by this 1937 Brazilian edition translated into Portuguese.

believed to be part of the *Protocols* plot.[4] Many years later, after Hitler came to power, the Nazis put up a monument to these "heroic young martyrs."[5]

*The Protocols of the Learned Elders of Zion*, because it was so widely believed, would be a major influence on all those who participated in the slaughter of the Jews, including anti-Semites from other nations as well as German Nazis.

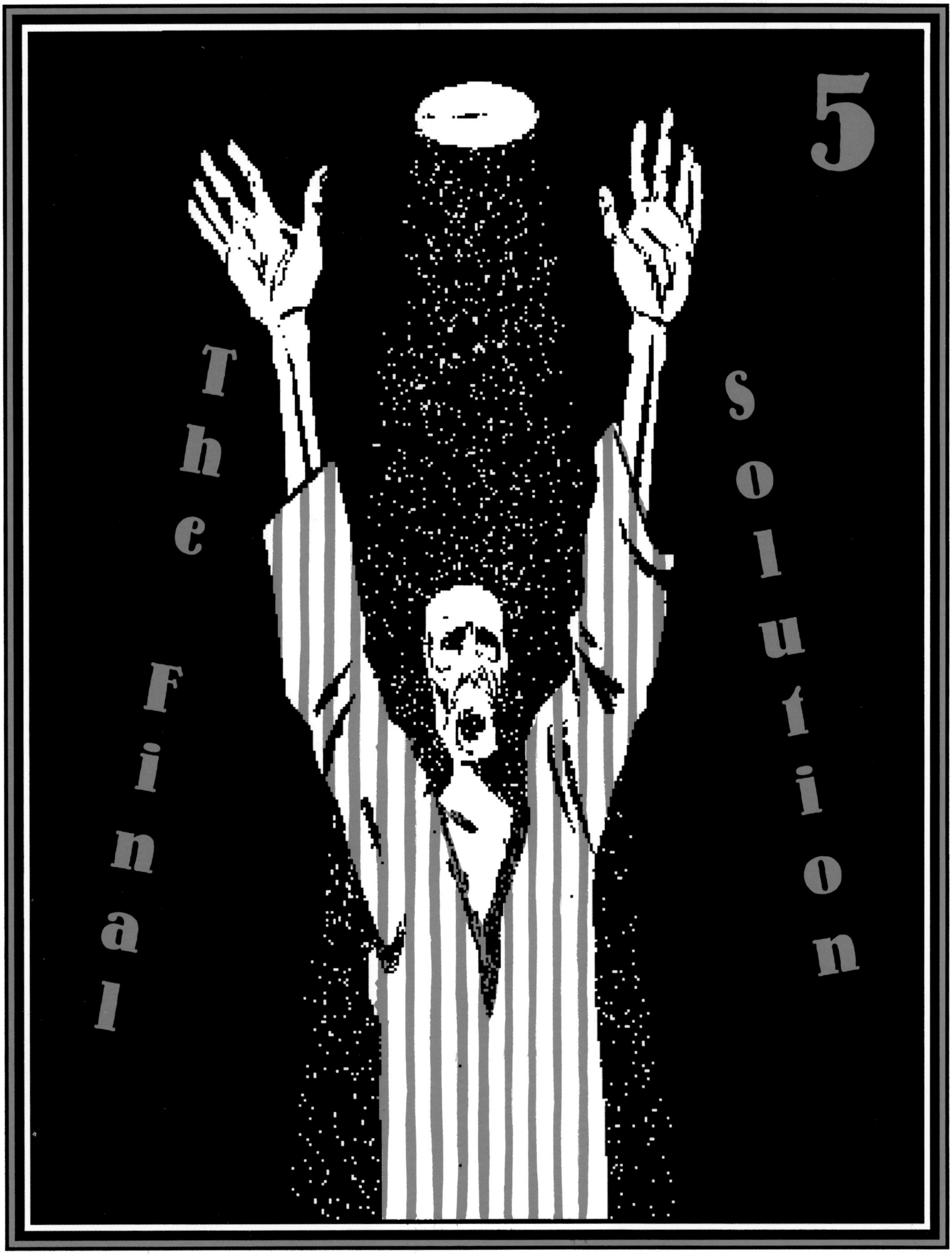
5
The Final Solution

*During the summer and fall of 1942, several hundred thousand Jews were massacred in the Volhynian-Podolian region [in Ukraine]. When the Germans entered a small ghetto and lined up its Jews, a little girl asked: "Mother, why did you make me wear the Shabbat dress; we are being taken out to be shot." The shooting site was on a hill about 2 miles (3 km) away, and the mother, carrying the child, was forced to run this distance after a truck already filled with victims. Standing near the dugout half-filled with bodies, the child said: "Mother, why are we waiting, let us run!" Some of the people who attempted to escape were caught immediately and shot on the spot. The mother stood there facing the grave. A German walked up to the woman and asked: "Whom shall I shoot first?" When she did not answer, he tore her daughter from her hands. The child cried out and was killed."* [1]

Testimony of the mother, Rivka Yosselevska, May 8, 1961, Eichmann trial transcript. . . . Yosselevska, wounded, crawled out of the pit. Small children, also wounded, escaped from the grave as well but, not knowing where to go, were rounded up and shot. [2]

O n September 1, 1939, German troops stormed across the Polish border and World War II began. On September 21, the Nazis issued an order that all Polish Jews were to be rounded up and forced into ghettos and other specified areas. There were roughly 3.35 million Jews in Poland at that time.

Some of them already lived in poor city neighborhoods known as ghettos. Others were scattered throughout the cities in middle-class and a few upper-class neighborhoods. Still others lived in towns and villages throughout Poland, some in so-called shtetlach where Jews lived apart from the Poles, some mixed in with the Polish small-town populations. Many Jewish families had lived among the Poles for hundreds of years.

Some of these Jews were merchants, some were dairy farmers, and some worked in small clothing factories owned by other Jews. The Poles came into contact with them every day. Sometimes their children played together. The women exchanged greetings in marketplaces. The men discussed the events of the day. Even in places where the Jews were set apart from the Poles, a certain amount of daily contact took place.

Nevertheless, during the roundups, some Jews were identified to the Nazis by their Polish neighbors. These neighbors took over their homes and property and businesses. There were exceptions—Poles who shielded the Jews, protected them, hid them, helped them escape—but many either turned their backs on the Jews or actively participated in these first steps of their destruction. The same would be true throughout Eastern Europe and in some Western European countries as well.

## Death by the Thousands

The herding of the Polish Jews took place in the winter of 1939–1940. Conditions were brutal. The Jews were forced to march through bitter winds and driving snows, often at temperatures about -40°F (-40°C). The very old and the very young were forced to endure these marches. Infants and old people died by the thousands. Those who couldn't keep up were shot by their Nazi guards.

When the survivors arrived at the ghettos in the cities or in the new labor camps, they were in very bad shape. Nothing had been done to prevent diseases in these places, and many fell ill with tuberculosis and typhoid. These were the first of many epidemics that would sweep over the ghettos and the labor camps.

Besides the Polish Jews, two other categories of Jews ended up in the ghettos and labor camps. The first were those Jews who had fled east from the Nazis in Germany, Austria, Czechoslovakia, Hungary, and Romania. These refugees had sought sanctuary in Poland and were trapped there along with the Polish Jews. The second were Jews rounded up in the countries of Central Europe by the Nazis between December 1939 and February 1940 and shipped to Poland, mostly to what would become known as the Lublin District.

During this period, tens of thousands of Jews were herded into the Lublin District. They spoke many different languages and often could not communicate with one another. They were all mixed together—factory workers and college professors, dairy farmers and lawyers, file clerks and department store owners, cab drivers, street cleaners, waiters and artists, writers and musicians. There were rabbis and Orthodox Jews; Jews who attended synagogue services only on the High Holy Days; and Jews who did not observe their religion at all.

There were old men with skullcaps, and young men who believed more in socialism or the new psychology of Sigmund Freud than in the Jewish religion. There were women who had been rich, poor, and middle class. There were infants, children of every age, and adolescents. Those with common interests clustered together, but on the whole the Jews forced together by the Nazis often had little in common with one another, other than that they were Jewish and therefore doomed.

To the Nazis, the Lublin District was "a place highly suited for the 'final solution of the Jewish problem.'"[3] Thousands more Jews were deported there during 1941 and the beginning of 1942. During this period, the Nazis completed their occupation of Western Europe and started their roundup of Jews in France, the Netherlands, Belgium, Norway, Yugoslavia, and Greece. In June 1941 the Nazi invasion of Russia began, and the Jews of Ukraine, Russia, Latvia, Lithuania, and Estonia also fell prey to the Nazis.

As more Jews arrived in the Lublin District, German companies began establishing factories and storage facilities there. Some 50,000 Jews became slave laborers in these places. The Nazis built the Majdanek concentration camp to house them. Later it would also house Russian soldiers taken prisoner during the war.

Both Russians and Jews would be starved and worked to death. Horrible as this was, it was only an opening chapter in the "final solution"—the Nazi program to exterminate all the Jews—for which plans were drawn up in July 1941. The Lublin District was to be a center for the mass extermination of European Jews.

## Death by Tens of Thousands

In the beginning, extermination squads in Poland, and later in Ukraine, Russia, Latvia, Lithuania, and Estonia followed the advance of the German army. They rounded up and executed Communists and Jews. At first this meant adult men, but later it was decided that "all Jews were . . . to be exterminated, without regard to age or sex."[4] These squads were made up of three groups: mobile SS units called *Einsatzgruppen*; Order Police made up of police units and civil servants from large German cities; and units of volunteers called *Schutzmannschaft* from other countries.

These extermination squads would swoop down on a village such as Jozefow in Poland and march the Jews who lived there into the village square. Able-bodied men would be separated out and shipped off to the slave labor camps of Lublin. The women, children, sick people, and old people left behind would then be killed. Of the 1,800 Jews in Jozefow, 900 were killed immediately. The numbers were far greater in other places.

One of the men in charge of such operations, the commander of *Einsatzkommando 3,* described how the mass killings were accomplished. "A site had to be selected and pits dug. The marching distance . . . to the pits averaged 4 to 5 kilometers [2.5 to 3 miles]. The Jews were brought to the place of execution in groups of 500, with a distance of at least 2 kilometers [1.2 miles] between groups. "[5]

Distance was kept between groups so that the Jews would not know their fate until the last minute. Sometimes the pits that would be mass graves were spaced between stands of trees so that the previous victims would not be seen. Usually, however, the Jews were not fooled.

At first the killing was done by individual soldiers using rifles. Nazi army doctors gave lectures on how to shoot most efficiently. They "outlined the contour of a human body . . . and then indicated precisely the point on which the fixed bayonet was to be placed as an aiming guide."[6]

Often the murders were done close up, one on one. A killer would be paired with his victim, sometimes two killers with two victims. One thirty-five-year-old member of the Order Police testified how this worked: "The mothers led the children by the hand. My neighbor then shot the mother and I shot the child that belonged to her, because I reasoned with myself that after all without its mother the child could not live any longer."[7]

# Death by Hundreds of Thousands

Executing large numbers of Jews in this way went too slowly to suit the Nazis. Adjustments were made to speed up the process. Firing squads were used. Machine guns replaced rifles. *Schutzmannschaft* battalions from Ukraine, Latvia, Lithuania, and Estonia were enlisted to speed up the killings and supplied with liquor so that they might go on shooting until they fell away from their guns in a drunken stupor.

The Jews were made to take off all of their clothes before they were killed. The Nazis realized that naked people put up less resistance. Also, it saved the killers the trouble of stripping the corpses of valuables. Redistributing the Jews' wealth among Aryans—no matter how small the items involved—was always an aim of the Nazis.

Some Jews tried to escape. Some fought back. Some pleaded for their lives. Some begged for the lives of their loved ones, their parents, their children, their babies. Many were fooled into cooperating right up to the very last minute. Some were terrified and thought that if they cooperated their lives might yet be spared.

Many went to their deaths gambling that the drunken shooters would miss and that they could pretend to be shot and make their escape from the mass graves later. A few did escape in this fashion. Others were killed by executioners moving through the graves with pistols and rifles to finish off those who were not yet dead. And some—nobody knows how many—were simply too stunned by the horror of their situation to think clearly, or to take any action at all.

Still the killings went too slowly for the Nazis. Around the end of 1941, gas vans were first used by the extermination squads. Up to 150 victims at a time could be locked in the vans' compartments and poisoned by carbon monoxide from the vans' exhaust pipes. This worked well where the vans stayed in one place and there were furnaces available to get rid of the bodies. There were

A woman facing execution at the Belzec concentration camp in Poland

problems, however, when the extermination squads moved hurriedly from place to place and had no way to dispose of so many corpses. Obviously, stationary gas chambers would be more efficient for killing the Jews.

## The Wannsee Conference

On December 16, 1941, Hans Frank, the Nazi governor-general of Poland, spoke to his top officials as follows: "About the Jews of Europe . . . the Jews have to disappear. They must go . . . liquidate them. . . ."[8]

A month later, on January 20, 1942, a conference of Nazis in charge of various branches of government met at Wannsee, a suburb of Berlin. The purpose of the meeting was to decide how to dispose of the remaining Jews of Europe most efficiently and speedily. Gestapo Chief Reinhard Heydrich explained the scope of the problem. "In the course of this final solution of the European Jewish problem," he told them, "approximately eleven million Jews are involved."[9]

He broke the figure down for them. Out of a quarter-million Jews in German territory in 1939, 131,800 were left. In Russia there were 5 million Jews, in Ukraine 3 million. In Poland 2.25 million were still alive. In France there were 750,000 Jews, and in Britain about 300,000.

To dispose of so many Jews would require a massive effort involving industry, transportation, the military, and the construction and operation of mass extermination centers. Seeing it through was a major aim of the Nazis. In the end it would become more important to the Nazis than winning the war.

## The Death Trains

During 1939 and 1940, tens of thousands of Austrian and German Jews had been shipped to the Lublin District. Beginning in March 1942, Jews from Latvia, Lithuania, and Ukraine began to be shipped there. At the same time, the death camps of Belzec, Sobibor and Treblinka were constructed. These were concentration camps outfitted with gas chambers for mass killings, and ovens for cremating the bodies of the victims.

Between March 25 and October 20, 1942, about 58,000 Jews were deported from Czechoslovakia (today the Czech Republic and Slovakia)—39,000 to the Lublin District, the rest to the Auschwitz concentration camp. Of those who reached the Lublin District, 24,500 were killed in Sobibor, 7,500 in Belzec, and 7,000 in Treblinka. In the spring of 1943, mass shipments of Jews from Greece and Yugoslavia (today Croatia and Bosnia) began. Starting in March 1942, with the cooperation of the French government, 75,000 Jews were sent to death camps from France. Between July 15, 1942, and September 3, 1944, Holland shipped 105,000 Jews in 98 trains to the death camps of Auschwitz, Sobibor, Theresienstadt, and Bergen-Belsen.

The journeys were horrible. Many Jews died before they ever reached the death camps and the gas chambers. Mostly, they suffocated. Holocaust survivor Abraham Goldfarb described how more than twice as many people as a freight car might reasonably be expected to hold were jammed in for the trip to Treblinka: "The cars were closed from the outside with boards. Water and food were not provided. People were suffocating; there was no air to breathe. . . . There were 150 people in our freight car. During the two-day trip to Treblinka, 135 suffocated."[10]

## The Killing Machine

The gas ovens and furnaces awaited those who survived the journeys to the death camps. War production had been put aside by major German manufacturing companies to provide the gas chambers, the furnaces, the forklifts to handle large numbers of corpses, the pumps and pipes for the gas, the mechanized digging equipment for the graves, and all of the other items used in the course of mass killings. The gas used in the killings was Zyklon-B (hydrogen cyanide).

Zyklon-B worked faster than carbon monoxide and other gases that had been tried, and its results were less horrible, which made the corpses easier to handle. It had first been tried on Russian prisoners of war at Auschwitz (a serious violation of international law). They died quickly, so Zyklon-B was adopted for use by most of the death camps.

The first gassings were overseen by doctors and other medical personnel who had been involved in the German Euthanasia Program in 1939–1940. The first commander of the Treblinka death camp was a doctor from that program. Those who ran the camp on a daily basis—guards, technicians, clerical staff—were German and Austrian SS men and Ukrainian, Latvian, and Lithuanian volunteers. Some of these were on hand to receive the Jewish survivors of the death trains. Usually there would also be a doctor there to meet the Jews when they were let out of the freight cars. The doctor separated those fit for work from those who were immediately sent to their deaths.

## The Selection Process

Jews were sometimes met with brutality when they arrived at the camps. They were forced to pass through twin lines of guards wielding clubs. Men, women, children, infants, old people—all were beaten at random. Already dazed from their ordeal, trying to cling to their loved ones, they were struck and ordered to go this way or that, sometimes in languages they did not understand.

At other death camps the arrivals were more orderly. Men, women, and children were separated into groups without brutality. The children would be led off. The doctors would make quick judgments, not really examinations. Women who were pregnant, ill, old, or particularly frail would be taken away. Next the elderly and the sick among the men would leave. In the end only a small group of able-bodied men and an even smaller group of women would remain. They would be led to the work camps to take the place of those who had already been worked to death or who showed signs of weakening.

The others were led, group by group, to buildings or yards where they were made to strip naked. Sometimes the Jewish women's hair was cut off by other women who had been spared for that purpose. Then they were told they were being taken to the showers—a welcome message after the freight cars—and were herded into the gas chambers. If they looked up, they could see false shower heads in the ceilings. If they listened after the doors had closed behind them, they could hear the hiss of the gas escaping.

Some of those Jews who had come through the initial selection process alive were made to deal with the results of the slaughter. They had to remove the corpses from the gas chambers and pile them on the forklifts that would shovel them into the furnaces. They had to sort out the belongings left behind, wash the clothing, and pack up items that could be sent back to Germany for warmth against the winter cold. They had to separate out any items of value they found. Before they had been put aboard the death trains, the Jews were told that they were being relocated and should take their valuables with them. Therefore, large amounts of jewelry and other items worth money were accumulated in the death camps.

Some of the dead bodies that the Jewish death camp workers dealt with were diseased. Sometimes the workers caught these diseases. They, too, were killed to keep the disease from spreading. Often, however, that did not work. Other inmates and even guards were infected. There were occasional epidemics.

## Death by the Millions

The Nazis in charge of the larger death camps tried to outdo each other. In Treblinka, 80,000 Jews were killed over a six-month period. During three months, 93,000 Jews were murdered in Belzec. At Treblinka it took only two months to kill 254,000 Jews from Warsaw. The commander of Auschwitz boasted of gassing 6,000 Jews a day.

The horror was often too much for the Jews in the camps who had not yet been killed. Some lost faith in life itself. At Treblinka, Abraham Lindwaser was assigned to pull gold teeth from the corpses he had helped remove from the gas chambers. It pushed him over the edge:

"I couldn't stand it. I tried to commit suicide. I was already hanging from the belt. A bearded Jew took me down. . . . He began lecturing me . . . we would have to make an effort so that at least someone would remain who could tell what was going on there, and that was my job . . ."[11]

It became the job of all who survived the death camps. It became a task not only for Jews but for all civilized people. The slaughter of all those the Nazis called *Untermenschen* could not be allowed to fade from memory.

# 6 The Fate of Other *Untermenschen*

fter the Jews, the main group viewed as *Untermenschen* by the Nazis was the Slavs. They included the Russians and Ukrainians of Eastern Europe, the Serbs and Slovenes of southern Europe, and the Czechs, Poles, and Slovaks of central Europe, all of whom are Slavic peoples. Hitler deemed that they "had no right to live, except . . . as slaves of their German masters."[1]

The first Slavs to be conquered by Nazi armies were those of Czechoslovakia in March 1939. On October 15, 1940, Hitler laid out a plan for them. Half were to be shipped to Germany to provide slave labor. The other half, particularly "intellectuals," were to be "eliminated."[2]

About the same time, Hitler had decided that since the Poles were "born for low labor," it followed that "the laborers needed by the Reich [the German nation] could be procured from there." He added that "the Polish gentry . . . must be exterminated," as well as Polish intellectuals. "There should be one master only for the Poles" and that is "the German," Hitler declared.[3]

As the conquering armies moved east, Erich Koch, the Nazi put in charge of Ukraine, spelled out the policy for the population of the region: "We are a master race, which must remember that the lowliest German worker is racially and biologically a thousand times more valuable than the population here."[4]

In the autumn of 1941, *Reichsmarschall* Hermann Göring, the number two Nazi, predicted that "this year between twenty and thirty million persons will die of hunger in Russia. Perhaps," he added, "it is well that it should be so."[5]

Two years later, SS Chief Heinrich Himmler was concerned that if the Russians "starve to death like cattle," they would not be available "as slaves to our *Kultur* [culture]." He added that "whether ten thousand Russian females fall down from exhaustion while digging an antitank ditch interests me only in so far as the antitank ditch for Germany is finished."[6]

## Slave Laborers

It wasn't just idle talk. Between the September 1939 invasion of Poland and September 1944, more than 7.5 million civilians from many countries were rounded up for shipment to Germany to work as slave laborers. Groups of people leaving movie theaters or coming out of churches were caught up in sudden raids. Wives and husbands were separated, and older children were kidnapped.

Nazi roundups of Russian civilians for slave labor were particularly brutal. At the postwar Nuremberg trials of Germans and others accused of committing crimes against humanity, a Nazi document describing one such roundup was read:

"The order came to supply twenty-five workers, but no one reported. Then the German militia came and began to set fire to the houses of those who had fled. . . . People who hurried to the scene . . . were beaten and arrested. . . . The militia went through the adjoining villages and seized laborers. . . . We are now catching humans like dog catchers used to catch dogs."[7]

In occupied Russia an order went out "to apprehend forty to fifty thousand youths from the age of ten to fourteen . . . and transport them to the Reich."[8] One purpose of the order was to deprive the enemy of present and future soldiers. The Nazis would work these young people to death to reduce the "biological potentialities [ability to have children]" of the Russians.[9]

Slave laborers were transported in sealed boxcars with no food, water, or toilet facilities for journeys that took two or three days and sometimes longer. Like the Jews being shipped to the death camps, many of them died there. A German doctor reported that some of the people who died had tuberculosis or venereal diseases that might spread.

Those who survived were put to work in German and Austrian coal mines and factories and on farms. They were underfed to the point of starvation, and they were beaten. Some died from the beatings and from lack of food. There was a shortage of shoes, and slave laborers were forced to work barefoot. Many had no coats and no blankets and died from exposure to the cold. Many more were simply worked to death.

## The Siege of Leningrad

It was as bad, or worse, for those who escaped the slave labor roundups. This was particularly true in Russia, where Göring's prediction of large numbers of people starving to death was coming true.

On September 8, 1941, the German army surrounded Leningrad, the second-largest city in Russia and an important port on the Baltic Sea. The German navy sealed off the harbor. It was the start of a siege in which the city was constantly bombarded by cannon fire, while food and medical supplies were prevented from reaching it. The siege lasted until January 27, 1944—872 days.

The winters of the siege were the worst. There was no fuel for heat. People burned their furniture to keep warm. There were epidemics of scurvy, dystrophy, and diarrhea. Corpses piled up in the streets. People did not move the dead, afraid that if they touched them they might catch whatever disease had killed them.

Food was rationed, but the rations were cut again and again. It was not enough to sustain life. People ate their shoes, their lipsticks, their pets, even the rats in the streets. There were cases of cannibalism.

A woman of Leningrad named Yelena Skryabina kept a diary. She wrote about her sixteen-year-old son, who once had been an active youth, but "now he was like an old man. . . . Unless he could be shaken from apathy, he would die.

It looks like a normal street scene in Leningrad, Russia, until the body being pulled on the sled is noticed. During the German siege of the city, which lasted well over two years, more than a million citizens died of starvation, disease, or exposure.

. . . He got only a child's ration of 200 grams [7 ounces] a day—a couple of slices of bread."[10]

She described how she made a jellied pâté by boiling old leather, and created a soup from cellulose to feed him. But it was very hard to hold on to hope when there was no food to give one strength. "Today it is so simple to die," she wrote. "You just begin to lose interest, then you lie on the bed and you never again get up."[11]

Many of those who died were killed by the shells that rained down on the city for more than two years. Others froze to death in the subzero winters. Most died from scurvy and starvation. All together, more than a million people, the great majority of them civilians, died during the siege of Leningrad.

## The Night and Fog Decree

In Russia, as in all of the occupied countries, civilian hostages were killed as punishment for guerrilla actions against the Nazis. This was official policy, and it was stated over and over again. Shortly before the Russian invasion, German Field Marshal Wilhelm Keitel had ordered that "collective drastic measures" should be taken against civilian populations when attacks against Germans had been made by unknown persons.[12]

Three months after the invasion of Russia, Keitel took note of "widespread guerrilla warfare" against German forces in occupied areas and recommended "the death penalty for fifty to a hundred Communists . . . as suitable atonement for one German soldier's death." The order specified that "troops are therefore authorized . . . to take any measures without restriction even against women and children. . . ."[13]

In December 1941, Hitler issued the Night and Fog Decree, which would be used against civilians in all the Nazi-occupied countries with increasing viciousness as the war continued. The decree authorized secret abduction of civilians. It specified that neighbors, friends, and families were to be given no information regarding the victims' sudden disappearance.

A boy coming home from school, a housewife-mother cleaning her home, a minister calling on the sick, a factory worker on his lunch break—these and others would simply vanish. When those who were left behind went to the authorities, even to the Gestapo, their queries went unanswered. Were their loved ones alive or dead? Weeks, months, and sometimes years went by with no word of their fate. In most cases, the families would never know what had happened to those who had disappeared. By creating this uncertainty, the Nazis deliberately "made life a torment of anxiety" for the civilians in occupied countries such as France, Holland, Norway, Czechoslovakia, Poland, and Russia.[14]

In fact, those who had been taken were either shot immediately or sent to the gas chambers of the death camps. Very few survived. But their loved ones never learned of their deaths, and so kept on asking what had happened to them.

Hitler himself provided the answer. "They disappeared into the night and fog," he said.[15]

## The Lidice Massacre

In contrast to those abducted secretly under the Night and Fog Decree, most reprisals were carried out publicly in order to discourage anti-Nazi opposition. The most infamous took place in the Czechoslovakian village of Lidice in June 1942, after SS General Reinhard Heydrich had been killed there by Czech underground resistance fighters. Nazi revenge was swift.

German soldiers surrounded the village. A Czech government report described what happened next: "A twelve-year-old boy tried to escape; a soldier shot him on the spot." The men of the village were locked in a barn. Later they "were led out . . . in batches of 10, and shot. The murders lasted from early morning until 4:00 in the afternoon." Nearly 200 men and older boys were killed. Later, seven women were killed. "The remaining 195 women were deported to the Ravensbruck concentration camp. . . . Four of these women were [first] taken from Lidice to a maternity hospital in Prague where their newly born infants were murdered; then the mothers were sent to Ravensbruck. The children of Lidice were taken from their mothers. . . . No trace of these children has been found."[16]

The village itself was plowed under and left as an empty field.

## Atrocity in France

Reprisals were equally harsh in the Western European countries occupied by the Nazis. The destruction of the French village of Oradour-sur-Glane was particularly vicious. It followed a report by a French Nazi collaborator that explosives used by guerrillas were hidden in the village.

The entire population was herded into the village square. The men were led off to five or six barns and locked inside them. The women and children were locked in a church. All the houses in the village and the surrounding countryside were set afire. As they burned, the men were led out of the barns and mowed down with machine guns.

German soldiers entered the church and set up an apparatus that discharged fumes. The air became unbreathable. When those in the church broke open a door in order to get air, the soldiers began shooting into the church. When the women and children in the church had been killed, it was burned to the ground. The soldiers then forced a passing train to halt, took the passengers off it, and machine-gunned them.

Those who died at Oradour-sur-Glane numbered 190 men, 245 women, and 207 children. Out of a population of 652 people, only 10 survived. The village was never rebuilt.

## Casualties of War

Killing unarmed civilians as revenge for anti-Nazi activity continued throughout the war. In Poland, Governor-General Hans Frank ordered that "when a

German is shot, up to a hundred Poles shall be shot too. . . ."[17] Just outside Paris the Germans used a suburban fort as a holding pen for hostages who were to be taken out and shot. When a Nazi officer in Nantes was killed, fifty hostages were shot and it was announced that fifty more would be shot if the assassin was not caught.

In Belgium five or more hostages were shot for every attack on a German soldier or policeman. In the Netherlands the most prominent people—nobles, statesmen, artists, writers, and so on—were held as hostages and executed. In Norway, when two German policemen were killed, eighteen young men were picked at random and executed. In Denmark there were "clearing murders" in which Nazi thugs took revenge after each act of resistance against the Nazis by murdering one or more innocent Danish citizens.[18]

The Nazi terrorists executed 267 hostages in Denmark, but Denmark is a small country. In the Netherlands, another small country, they killed 2,000 hostages. The numbers in Poland and France, countries about equal in size to Germany, are much higher. Hostage victims totaled 8,000 in Poland and 29,660 in France.

Hostage deaths, however, were only a small percentage of the civilian deaths caused by the Nazis. In France, for instance, some 40,000 people died in prisons during the Nazi occupation. Poland lost a higher percentage of its population (17.2 percent including military casualties) than any other country that fought in the war. In actual numbers, however, the Russians suffered the worst losses. About 15 to 20 million Russian civilians and soldiers died in World War II. Many of them died from disease, starvation, and exposure to the winter cold. Some 3.5 million Germans also died. They, too, might be considered victims of the Nazi effort to establish an Aryan master race.

Among those murdered were large numbers of Gypsies. Indeed, the Gypsies were "a group whose extermination the SS pursued with almost the same determination as that of the Jews."[19] But the Gypsies were not *Untermenschen*. They were descended from the same people as the Germans. The Gypsies were Aryans.

# 7

# The Aryans That Aryans Slaughtered

*I remember what happened in the "night of the gypsies." . . .*
*That night will remain with me as long as I live. Throughout the*
*kingdom of the night a whisper of fire ran through from man to*
*man, from child to child. We heard just one word—*
*they are burning the Gypsies.*[1]

Death camp survivor Elie Wiesel

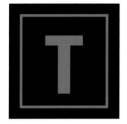he Gypsies are part of the Indo-European Aryan race of northern India. They came to Europe at the beginning of the fifteenth century, spreading out from the Balkan Peninsula into Germany, Austria, Czechoslovakia, Hungary, and the lands to the east. They were called Gypsies because the Europeans confused them with the Egyptians who were part of the Muslim army that had once invaded Europe. They call themselves *Romany*.

They were—and are—different from other Europeans. The Romany have been a nomadic people, often moving from one place to another. Some of these moves were because they were traders and peddlers who bought and sold as they traveled. Some Gypsy groups wandered in search of work. Some moved on because the local people drove them out.

Prejudice against Gypsies in Western countries came from their being so different. They had different customs and different practices and spoke a different language. They dressed differently, kept to themselves, did not go to local churches, and did not let their children attend local schools. One major reason for the bigotry against them was that they had much darker skin than the average European.

Non-Gypsies regarded the Romany as all the same. They were not. They were composed of many different tribes, each separate from the others. These tribes each had different customs and beliefs. They spoke different dialects.

Each had a different leader. In a sense, they were like the Native American tribes of North America—wandering groups as distinct from one another as from the populations among whom they moved.

## "Worthless Life"

The Romany were Aryans, just as the Germans were. But this did not prevent them from being persecuted in Germany soon after their arrival there. Indeed, the first anti-Gypsy law was passed in Germany in 1416. Forty-eight such laws were passed over the next 350 years.

In more modern times, even before Hitler came to power, laws targeting Gypsies were passed in both Germany and Austria. During this period and later, the Nazis, unable to deny that the Gypsies were Aryans, had to find some reason other than racial purity for persecuting them. They did this by defining the Gypsies as "asocial elements"—outcasts from normal society. The Nazis said that the Gypsies "endangered the purity of Aryan blood and the public health."[2]

As early as 1920, both a German psychiatrist and a prominent legal expert were including Gypsies among those they labeled "worthless life."[3] Their opinions would be acted upon when the Nazis came to power. "Worthless life" would be snuffed out; Gypsies would be eliminated.

In 1928, Germany was still a republic ruled by the Weimar constitution, which guaranteed equal rights to all. Despite this, a law was passed putting all Gypsies under permanent police scrutiny. The following year the police started putting Gypsies over the age of sixteen in "rehabilitation camps." Then, in 1933, when the Nazis came to power, the Sterilization Law was passed. "Lives not worthy of life" were defined as "specifically Gypsies and most of the Germans of black color."[4]

Over the next three years, Gypsies rounded up for sterilization were sent to concentration camps at Belzec, Dachau, Sachsenhausen, Dieselstrauss, Marzahn, and Vennhausen. New laws were passed that forbade Gypsies to

Gypsy prisoners at Belzec, about 1941

marry Germans. In Austria the "International Center for Combating the Gypsy Menace" was established.[5]

Activity against the German Gypsies increased in 1938 with large-scale roundups and construction of a new camp at Buchenwald. Gypsies from the Rhineland, Austria, and Czechoslovakia were shipped there by the Nazis. An SS study group urged "the mass drowning of Gypsies in boats to be towed out to sea and sunk."[6] There was no follow through on the suggestion.

## The Mass Killings Begin

On September 27, 1939, less than a month after World War II began, Hitler ordered German Gypsies shipped to camps in Poland. Supply trains for the German army waited on sidings, while freight cars "packed with Gypsies" moved east. The German Office of Racial Hygiene declared that the aim of the campaign to rid Germany of Gypsies was "elimination without hesitation of this defective element in the population."[7]

Meanwhile, at Buchenwald, 250 Gypsy children were being used as guinea pigs in the first experiments to test Zyklon-B, the gas later mass-produced for use in the death camps. In July 1941, the *Einsatzkommandos* in Poland were ordered to kill all Gypsies as well as Jews. Some 5,000 Gypsies were sent with 20,000 Jews to the Lódz ghetto where a typhus epidemic killed many of them within a few months. Those who survived were sent to the Chelmno extermination camp for execution.

Thousands of Gypsies were forced to join the Jews in the Warsaw ghetto. To tell them apart, they were forced to wear armbands with the letter Z for *Zigeuner* ("Gypsy" in German). They eventually were sent to Treblinka. More than 2,000 Gypsies died at Treblinka. On December 16, 1942, Heinrich Himmler, who was head of the SS, ordered all remaining Gypsies in areas controlled by the Nazis to be sent to concentration camps. A special section for Gypsies was set up at Auschwitz. More than 20,000 Gypsies, most of them from Germany, were gassed there.

## The Gypsies of Serbia and Croatia

Not all the Gypsies were sent to concentration camps. As the plague of Nazi occupation armies spread over Europe, the large-scale killing of Gypsies often occurred without the bother of shipping them to death camps. This happened in Yugoslavia, which the Nazis separated into two territories after they conquered the country.

The two areas were Croatia and Serbia. In Serbia, where guerrillas constantly attacked the occupying forces, the Nazi military carried out a policy of killing one hundred Gypsies, Communists, and Jews for every German soldier killed, and of executing fifty for every German soldier wounded. In less than a year, Berlin was notified that "Serbia is the only country in which the Jewish and Gypsy questions have been solved."[8] On November 13, 1942, a Belgian newspaper confirmed that all the Gypsies in Serbia had been killed.

In Croatia, government officials actively cooperated with the Nazis. The Croats considered themselves Aryans like the Germans. Here, a puppet government run by Croats had been set up by the Nazis. This government ran 22 concentration camps in which 28,500 Gypsies—99 percent of the Croatian Gypsy population—were murdered.

## Victims and Survivors

The prewar Nazi occupation had divided Czechoslovakia as well. The western portion of the country—Bohemia and Moravia—was ruled directly by the German Nazis. Slovakia, however, became an "independent" puppet state of the Nazis.[9] The Gypsies of Bohemia and Moravia were wiped out, but most of those in Slovakia survived.

In tiny Albania, where the Italian army was replaced by the Germans late in the war, the survival rate for Gypsies was high. In Greece, they were taken hostage by the hundreds and shot. In 1943 an order was issued that Greek Gypsies were to be rounded up and sent to Auschwitz for execution. The Greek prime minister and Greek Archbishop Damaskinos protested and the order was canceled—as in Denmark and Bulgaria, where firm resistance to Nazi racial policies got results.

For the most part, the Gypsies of east-central and Eastern Europe were not so fortunate. In Latvia, some Gypsies were rounded up and shot. Others were deliberately starved to death. Approximately 28,000 to 32,000 Hungarian Gypsies were murdered. Between 36,000 and 39,000 Romanian Gypsies died under Nazi rule. However, in Bulgaria, which was a German ally during the war, Nazi anti-Gypsy policies, like those against the Jews, were for the most part not enforced.

Only about 5,500 of Poland's 19,000 prewar Gypsy population survived. These were Romany tribes who had long lived in the forests, where they had developed skills that helped them escape the Nazi death squads. Some formed themselves into underground resistance bands. But these Romany did not join up with other Polish resistance groups out of fear of being turned over to the Nazis. It should be mentioned that—unlike the experience of the Jews—there is no evidence that Poles or Ukrainians ever betrayed the Gypsies.

Nevertheless, in Ukraine and Russia, Gypsies suffered high losses. They were either shot immediately by *Einsatzgruppen* extermination squads or shipped to death camps in Poland. No Gypsies survived the death camps of Belzec, Chelmno, Majdanek, Sobibor, or Treblinka.

## Mengele the Candy Man

During the first half of the 1940s, a variety of medical experiments were being performed on Gypsies at Dachau, Buchenwald, and Auschwitz. Dr. Josef Mengele was in charge of the program at Auschwitz. One of his projects was to come up with a method to change seawater into drinking water. Gypsies at Sachsenhausen were forced to drink salt water over a period of weeks to see how long they could survive on it. Most drank until they drowned and died. Both men and women were used in these experiments.

Another Mengele project involved Romany twins. He would roam the Gypsy section of Auschwitz paying particular attention to the children. They were starving, and he gave them candy. When he found twins among the Romany children, he would take them back to his laboratory and have them killed "in order to make a special comparative 'study' of Gypsy and Aryan eye coloration."[10]

## Countless Thousands Mourn

Dr. Mengele escaped from Germany after the war and lived out his life in South America. Contrast this with the fate of the European Gypsies. Prewar population figures of Gypsies are hard to pin down, and so are the actual numbers of those killed. However, some Holocaust scholars have made estimates.

Simon Wiesenthal, head of the world-renowned Simon Wiesenthal Center, which hunts down former Nazis and brings them to justice, believes that 80 percent of Europe's Gypsies were slaughtered by the Nazis. Other Holocaust specialists estimate that "1 million to 4 million [Gypsies] died."[11] We may never know the actual number of victims, but surely the fate of the Gypsies during the Holocaust demonstrates the truth of the words of poet Robert Burns when he wrote:

*Man's inhumanity to man*
*Makes countless thousands mourn.*[12]

# The Pink Triangle

**8**

omosexuals are men and women who are attracted to those of their own sex. They exist in every society. In some they have been accepted and respected. In most, they have not. This has often kept them "in the closet"—which means that they have kept their homosexuality secret.

Today, in the United States, attitudes toward homosexual men and women are improving. This is also true in Europe, including Germany. The climate there is far different from what it was throughout the Nazi era. During those years homosexuals faced death.

## The Making of Criminals

After Hitler justified the 1934 killing of Nazi leader Ernst Röhm and his key lieutenants because of their homosexuality, the Gestapo directed all Regional Criminal Police Bureaus to compile "lists of persons who had been homosexually active." The Gestapo was especially interested "in their membership [in] Nazi organizations."[1] Nazi homosexuals were considered potential traitors like Röhm.

In March 1935, Berlin police raided pubs patronized by homosexuals. Of the 1,770 men caught in the sweep, 413 were held in "preventive detention" on trumped-up charges.[2] Later, 325 of these were sent to a concentration camp.

Magazines slanted toward homosexuals had to cease publication. When a judge sentenced several homosexuals to prison under local laws and there were protests, he warned that in the future any kind of homosexual activity would be punished. By June 1935, the Nazis had added an amendment to the national Penal Code defining homosexuality as a criminal activity.

## The Plague

The Penal Code amendment said that it was a crime if one man touched another "with sexual intent."[3] It declared that "whoever commits an act" offensive to "the basic principle of . . . healthy public feeling" would be punished.[4] Thus, the law was now expanded to cover vague "moral offenses," as well as sex offenses.[5]

Besides names provided by the police, the Gestapo seized membership records from homosexual associations. These records provided "over two million names."[6] The number alarmed high-ranking Nazi Heinrich Himmler.

Himmler formed the Reich Office for the Combating of Homosexuality and Abortion. He described its mission to high-ranking SS officers on February 18, 1937: ". . . we have 67 to 68 million people in Germany . . . approximately 20 million sexually capable men (males above the age of sixteen). . . . Assuming one to two million homosexuals, the result is that roughly 7–8 percent of men in Germany are homosexual. . . . our nation will fall to pieces because of that plague."[7]

## Homosexual Husbands

During the following months special mobile Gestapo units carried out arrest sweeps of homosexuals in small towns throughout Germany. "Preventive detention" became more and more widespread.[8] It was not always even-handed. On October 29, 1937, for example, Himmler issued an order that "any

These prisoners at the Sachsenhausen camp in Germany wear the triangular badges that indicate their homosexuality, the reason for their imprisonment.

detention of an actor or artist for unnatural sex acts" required his personal "prior approval."[9]

Many homosexuals married to conceal their homosexuality. Himmler saw the "greatest danger" of homosexual men "driving their wives to adultery (a million according to Himmler's figure)." Since maintaining a high Aryan birthrate was a principal Nazi aim, he feared that homosexual husbands, by not having sex with their wives, were "blocking" their ability to bear children. On the other hand, if they had marital relations, Himmler feared the children would be born "eugenically inferior"—that is, homosexual like their fathers.[10]

## A Homosexual Remembers

One male homosexual who was twenty years old in 1937 wrote about life during the Nazi years: "During my youth . . . the homosexuals . . . ," he recalled, "were 'degenerates' to be beaten up at will. Doing so, even the lowest, most rotten, pathetic thug could feel great."[11]

When the war began, he became a medical corpsman. He met a young doctor, "an oddly tormented individual. One day he disappeared." Months later, assigned to a stockade where military prisoners were held, he ran into the doctor. "He was only a shadow of his former self, a skeleton. I was deeply shocked, in despair about not being able to help. I never saw him again."[12]

It was an awakening. "The Nazis did drive our people [homosexuals] even deeper into illegality," he wrote. "Many were murdered in their barbaric camps. Yet despite all that, there existed in that era what today is called a 'scene.'"[13]

The scene existed mostly in large cities. Word of mouth guided homosexuals to certain gathering places such as pubs, taverns, private clubs, indoor swimming pools, cafeterias, and amusement centers. In such areas, homosexuals identified themselves to each other by signals such as a red bandanna hanging out of a back pocket.

Both the police and the Gestapo raided these areas frequently. Some places catering to homosexuals were closed down permanently. A few kept managing to reopen.

Unofficially, the Gestapo allowed this. It made it easier to round up homosexuals in groups, rather than hunt down individuals. They didn't have to look for new homosexual hangouts. In particular, it made it easier to capture closeted homosexuals on leave from the military.

## A Variety of Punishments

Homosexuals in the military had to keep their sexual preference secret. Only when they went on leave could they seek out places where they could be themselves. But if they were caught in them, they faced court-martial.

Between September 1939 and July 1944, about 7,000 homosexuals in the German armed services were prosecuted. In August 1941, Hitler personally called for "ruthless severity" toward homosexuals in the military, the Nazi party, and the Hitler Youth organization.[14] Three months later the death penalty was ordered for homosexuals in the SS and in the police.

There were different laws for homosexual civilians. In January 1942, number two Nazi Hermann Göring ordered "detention in perpetuity in a penal camp" [a life sentence] for "sex offenses between men."[15] However, before detention, civilian homosexuals were offered the possibility of release if they made a "voluntary decision for castration"—removal of their sex organs by surgery.[16]

On November 14, 1942, the Nazi government ordered that all homosexuals who had been shipped to concentration camps were to be forcibly castrated. This included homosexuals in Buchenwald who had been there since the roundups of the mid-1930s. Some of them were used in experiments in the "Reversal of Hormonal Polarity," a research program based on the idea that homosexuality in men was a disease for which a cure could be found.[17]

Various drugs, surgery, and implants were tried out. Often anesthetics were not used, and there was extreme pain. One way or another, all the men ended up castrated. Many of them died from the experiments. Many homosexual prisoners at Buchenwald also died painful deaths involving typhoid fever experiments.

## Life in the Death Camps

Homosexuals in the camps were identified by a pink cloth triangle. They were singled out for especially harsh treatment by the guards. They were often shunned by other prisoners who did not want to be considered homosexual, or who were prejudiced against homosexuals. They were deliberately separated from one another. The pink triangle system, however, didn't always work. Many homosexuals were able to simply take them off. Many avoided wearing them altogether in the camps.

Survivors described known homosexuals as "the lowest caste in the camp."[18] At every level of camp administration they were singled out for the harshest treatment. This was true even of camp doctors who treated other sick slave laborers but often gave ill homosexuals lethal injections. In many cases, doctors shipped homosexuals out to other camps to avoid treating them. "This constant moving of broken people had the result that they died off like flies with every change of conditions," one homosexual survivor remembered.[19]

## The Persecution of Women

Lesbians—homosexual women—were also singled out for special treatment in the camps. If they were Aryan, they were forced to become prostitutes in the brothels set up for German and Austrian personnel. This was considered not just a punishment but also a possible way of curing them of their homosexuality through frequent forced sex with men.

Those who were not Aryans were turned over to gangs of prisoners for forced sex. Seven non-Aryan lesbians were sent to the Bützow concentration camp where they were delivered to Russian and French war prisoners who were ordered to repeatedly rape them. The seven were kept apart from other women prisoners. Two died of starvation, one from tuberculosis. The fate of the other four is unknown. In other camps, lesbians were tormented and killed in experiments intended to "cure" homosexuality.

Only a small percentage of lesbians were sent to the camps because of their homosexuality. In Germany those lesbians who were arrested were charged with conduct "subversive of the military potential," which meant they were deliberately avoiding having children.[20] There is no telling how many lesbians became wives and mothers to avoid such charges.

The number of lesbians who died at the hands of the Nazis is not known. Estimates vary widely on the number of both female and male homosexuals killed by the Nazis between 1933 and 1945. Many who remained in the closet certainly were caught up in the various roundups of *Untermenschen* as the Nazis occupied country after country. Many who were openly homosexual may have been singled out for killing in these roundups as well. Estimates range from several hundred thousand to 1.5 million male and female homosexuals killed by the Nazis.

# 9
# Prisoners
# of
# War

The 1929 Geneva Convention Relating to the Treatment of Prisoners of War provided for the protection of prisoners. They were to be safeguarded "from violence, intimidation, insults . . ."[1] The international agreement, which Germany signed, stated that captors "must treat prisoners humanely."[2]

On October 18, 1942, Hitler issued a top-secret Commando Order that "all enemies on so-called commando missions . . . will be exterminated, without exception, to the last man."[3] If one or two were initially spared for questioning, "then they are to be shot immediately after interrogation." He added that "under no circumstances" were they "to be treated according to the rules of the Geneva Convention."[4]

Aware that this was a violation of international law, Nazi General Alfred Jodl instructed that the order "must not under any circumstances fall into enemy hands."[5]

## The Starvation Policy

Hitler's order only made official a Nazi policy of violating the Geneva Convention—a policy that was already in effect and taking a terrible toll. On the Eastern Front, 3.8 million Russian soldiers had been taken prisoner between June 21 and December 6, 1941. Nazi records show that many of these were deliberately starved and left outdoors in subzero cold to die.

"The more of these prisoners who die, the better it is for us," wrote Nazi Minister for the Occupied Eastern Territories Alfred Rosenberg. He reported that already "a large part of them have starved, or died . . ." although "there was food enough in Russia to provide for them."[6]

Death came more swiftly for other prisoners of war (POWs) on the Eastern Front. All Asian Russian POWs were shot. All Jewish Russian POWs were shot. All POWs identified (often wrongly) as Communist officials were shot.

## POW Slave Labor

As time passed, Hitler came to regret the slaughter of prisoners. Himmler expressed the Führer's concern about "the loss of labor" when "the prisoners died in tens and hundreds of thousands of exhaustion and hunger."[7] By November 1941, a total of five million prisoners of war taken from all the countries Germany had overrun were still alive. Four million were employed as slave labor in war industries. Most of these had been shipped to Germany and Austria, but now Göring had plans to set up "factories of armor and guns . . . also construction of parts for aircraft engines" in the occupied areas of Poland and Russia.[8] These were to be manned by Russian prisoners of war.

Coal was needed to run the factories for war production. A major source was the Saar region of Germany. More than 200,000 Russian POWs were shipped to German coal mines where they were underfed and overworked for years. Many died. They were constantly replaced by still more Russian POWs until the tide of war turned against the Germans.

The Geneva Convention forbade POWs to be used as labor to produce weapons for use against their own country. The Nazis disregarded this. One general was soon boasting that "our best new [warplane] engine is made 88 percent by Russian prisoners of war."[9]

Another Nazi commander, Field Marshal Erhard Milch, requested that 50,000 Russian POWs be put under his antiaircraft artillery command. "Thirty thousand are already employed as gunners," he reported. "It is an amusing thing that Russians must work the guns."[10]

The 100,000 French POWs assigned to the armaments industry in August 1941 also did jobs that were specifically forbidden by the Geneva Convention. They were used to move munitions, load bombs on planes, repair aircraft, dig trenches, and build bunkers. The few who protested were shot—supposedly for trying to escape.

## Don't Upset the People

Because of the conditions they had lived under before being shipped to Germany for forced labor, a high percentage of Russian POWs were weak and ill. They were then transported to nearby concentration camps to be killed. One problem this caused when they arrived alarmed a chief of the Gestapo. "When marching . . . from the railroad station to the camp, a rather large number of prisoners of war collapsed on the way from exhaustion, either dead or half dead, and had to be picked up by a truck following the convoy. It cannot be prevented that the German people take notice of these occurrences."[11]

There was a change of policy. POWs too sick to work were no longer transported to death camps to be executed. Instead, they were screened out and killed before being transported. It was more efficient.

Nor were Russian POWs the only ones murdered. Hitler ordered that in Yugoslavia all those who fought the Germans were to be treated as "bandits." On May 12, 1943, Major General Ludwig Kuebler ordered that all POWs were "to be shot after interrogation."[12]

## Torture and Death

"Interrogation" meant torture. Resistance fighters in all the conquered countries were covered by the Geneva Convention. The Nazis tortured and killed them anyway.

The evidence at the Nuremberg war crimes trials showed that treatment of guerrilla POWs in Western Europe could be as bad as in the east. "In Denmark . . . lashing with sticks or beating with rubber truncheons" was common. "Gestapo torture in Belgium left some men disfigured for life."[13] A witness described how a prisoner in France was forced to walk barefoot on tacks, was burned with cigarettes, and then was beaten until he died. In Oslo, Norway, torture interrogations caused fifty-two deaths.

Some torture was not to obtain information. POWs, like various civilians, were used in medical experiments in the concentration camps. One example involved burning Russian POWs at Buchenwald with phosphorus in order to try out different salves developed by the German chemical industry. Some relieved the agonizing burns. Some did not. Either way the horribly scarred prisoners were eventually killed.

## Execution of Prisoners

As the war drew to a close, the treatment of captured American and British soldiers and airmen became harsher. There was an unofficial secret policy to encourage German civilians to lynch bomber crews who bailed out over Germany. More often, the killings were carried out by the German military.

On the night of March 22, 1944, two U.S. commando officers and thirteen men—all in uniform—were captured behind German lines in Italy. They were executed by firing squad without trial, by order of General Anton Dostler. The general later said that he was obeying Hitler's Commando Order and that he would have been court-martialed if he had refused.

Increasingly, Hitler was becoming more directly involved in such murders. When fifty British fliers were recaptured after their escape from a POW camp in the spring of 1944, they were executed by direct order from Hitler. However, that wasn't really needed. Ordinary soldiers in the field were shooting prisoners. One such incident that particularly shocked Americans is remembered as the Malmédy Massacre.

## The Malmédy Massacre

On December 17, 1944, some German tanks came upon a group of unarmed American soldiers who had been taken prisoner during the Battle of the Bulge near Malmédy, Belgium. They were standing in a field, some with their hands raised high in the air. Others had their hands clasped behind their necks.

A German officer rose up out of the turret of his tank, took out his revolver, and deliberately fired into the group of prisoners. One fell to the ground. He fired again and a second dropped. Then two of the tanks opened fire with machine guns on the group. Most of the Americans were hit. The German tanks then moved off, leaving behind them a field littered with the dead, the dying, and the wounded.

Another group of German vehicles then drove past the field. They loosed several volleys of small-arms fire into the bodies—living and dead—lying in the field. Next came a group of German soldiers on foot. They "shot with pistol or rifle, or clubbed with a rifle butt or other heavy object, any of the American soldiers who still showed any sign of life."[14]

In all, seventy-one American soldiers who had already surrendered to the Germans were slaughtered at Malmédy.

## The Final Madness

By January 1945 the Geneva Convention was virtually ignored by the Nazis. By order of Dr. Ernst Kaltenbrunner, fifteen members of a British-American military mission, including an Associated Press reporter, were executed at Mauthausen concentration camp. In February, Goebbels suggested that word be spread that all captured Allied airmen would be shot in reprisal for bombing German cities.

Hitler agreed. He believed that if "I treat enemy prisoners without any consideration for their rights, regardless of reprisals, then quite a few [Germans]

Bodies of American prisoners of war killed at Malmédy, Belgium, are numbered, perhaps in the order in which they fell.

will think twice before they desert." Admiral Karl Dönitz disagreed. He convinced Hitler "to keep up outside appearances and carry out the measures believed necessary without announcing them beforehand."[15]

On April 22, 1945, just before Germany surrendered and the war ended, Gottlob Berger, head of Himmler's Prisoner-of-War Administration, went to Hitler's bunker to discuss the fate of a group of prominent British, French, and American POWs. Hitler's "face went bluish purple," according to Berger. "'Shoot them all! Shoot them all!'"[16] Hitler repeated over and over again.

One week later Adolf Hitler killed himself.

**10** Those Who Fought Back

*Do not go gentle into that good night;*
*Old age should burn and rave at close of day;*
*Rage, rage against the dying of the light.*

Dylan Thomas

hen the Nazis first came to power in Germany, wrote the late Yeshiva University Professor Lucy S. Dawidowicz, "the Jews demonstrated their defiance of the dictatorship by insisting on their rights."[1] After the Nuremberg Laws and *Kristallnacht*, that was no longer possible. They had no rights.

They were too few in number to fight, too concerned with the fate of children, elderly parents, and sick relatives to risk certain defeat. The Nazis wanted Germany *Judenrein*—free of Jews. Their message was clear: Either get out or stay and be killed.

But it was difficult to flee Germany. Jews had to leave their property behind. They were allowed to take only a small amount of money out of the country. It was hard to get exit visas, and often families were split apart. Other countries—including the United States—did not welcome Jewish refugees without money.

## Lists and Lies

Leaders of Jewish organizations stepped in to bring fairness and order to the situation. They drew up lists of Jews and assigned places to them. They worked out schedules for departures.

The Nazis encouraged this, but put up obstacles to keep it from working. They began using the lists provided by the Jewish leaders to round up the Jews. After the invasion of Russia, they began shipping tens of thousands of these German Jews to camps in Poland.

A variety of lies were told to make the victims cooperate. The Nazis announced that an agreement had been made with President Roosevelt to transfer the Jews to Madagascar. Then the Jews were told that they were being given land in Eastern Europe. Then they were told that they were being sent to new, clean labor camps. When the weak and sick were shot during forced marches to the railroad stations, the survivors counted themselves lucky to be strong enough to do the work. When they arrived at the camps, many believed they were being herded to take showers in the chambers where they were gassed. Those allowed to live were forced to write postcards to relatives still in Germany describing how pleasant conditions in the labor camps were.

## Hope and Disbelief

Hope was constantly held out to keep the victims passive. Colored tickets were distributed. Those with red tickets would be marched off to work, while those with green tickets would be killed. A few days later the greens would work and the reds would be killed. There was no pattern.

With choice came the hope of survival. The Nazis provided many such choices. But as time wore on, not many were fooled. Hope faded and the idea of resistance took hold.

At first the surviving Jews throughout occupied Europe could not believe that such large numbers of people were being killed. The truth spread through rumors, tales told by the few who escaped the camps, and stories in illegal underground newspapers. In April 1942, one such paper, the *Nowe Tory* ("New Tracks") of Warsaw, reported that "seven thousand people . . . deported to Belzec" had been "murdered with poisonous gas."[2] On September 20, another paper, *Oif der Vach* ("On Guard"), headlined the news that "The Jews of Warsaw Are Killed in Treblinka."[3]

These members of a youth resistance group from the Kovno ghetto in Lithuania represent the many organizations that sprang up in ghetto after ghetto in an effort to fight the Nazis.

# The Ghettos Fight Back

The news spread through all the ghettos. Disbelief gave way to shock, and resistance built slowly. The Nazis had all the power, the guns, and the troops, and often the cooperation of anti-Semites and other civilians eager to seize the property taken from Jews and Gypsies. Nevertheless, from 1943 on the Germans took casualties while rounding up victims.

In January 1943, a small group from the anti-Nazi underground of the Grodno ghetto slipped out to a nearby forest to buy guns from Poles. The effort failed. "There was no choice but to die honorably in the ghetto," wrote a member of the group.[4] They fought back with what they had—sometimes with their bare hands.

During the same month, in the Bialystok ghetto, a young underground leader named Mordecai Tenenbaum-Tamaroff released a manifesto to his people. "We have nothing to lose anymore!" he told them. "Jews, you are being led to Treblinka! They will poison us with gas . . . We do not want to go like sheep to slaughter!"[5]

They didn't. The February 1943 roundup of three thousand Bialystok Jews was accomplished only after nine hundred had died fighting the Germans. Homemade Molotov cocktails—jars filled with gasoline and sealed with wax in which a cotton fuse was embedded—were used to battle the armed Nazi troops. The Germans took heavy losses.

The following August, German and Ukrainian troops descended on Bialystok with orders to destroy the ghetto and either kill all the remaining Jews or ship them to death camps. Two Jewish youth groups fired on those guarding the prisoners awaiting the death trains. One was a squad of women led by a young woman named Mika Datner. They kept up an ongoing crossfire that sent the Germans running for cover. When it was over, among the resistance fighters who had been killed was the underground leader Mordecai Tenenbaum-Tamaroff.

# The Warsaw Ghetto

The best-known uprising took place in the Warsaw ghetto during the spring of 1943. Here, in 1940, about 400,000 people had been forced into a walled-in area 2.5 miles (4 km) long and 1 mile (1.6 km) wide. They were given one bowl of soup, sometimes boiled from straw, per person per day. This was part of a deliberate starvation policy. Two years later, between July 22 and October 3, 1942, more than 310,000 ghetto Jews were shipped to the death camps.

On April 19, 1943, the Germans launched a "special action" against the 60,000 Jews left alive in the ghetto.[6] They had been forced into an area measuring 1,000 yards (914 m) by 300 yards (274 m). Tanks, artillery, flamethrowers, and dynamite squads were ordered to clear them out and burn what was left of the ghetto to the ground. The operation was scheduled to take three days.

Resistance came from a variety of groups, including Zionists committed to establishing a Jewish nation in Palestine, Communists, Gypsies, the Jewish Combat Organization, and other bands that developed spontaneously as the battle developed. They fought from an area of cellars, sewers, strategic rooftops, and secret passages well suited for urban guerrilla warfare. They took on the Nazi military with smuggled guns and homemade bombs. All together they had "a few automatic weapons, some dozens of rifles, several hundred pistols, and a larger number of grenades and explosives. Stocks of ammunition were low."[7]

# Fierce Resistance

SS General Jürgen Stroop, in charge of the Nazi operation to destroy the Warsaw ghetto, reported: "We ran into strong concerted fire by the Jews . . . ." He mentioned damage to tanks from Molotov cocktails. "Owing to this enemy counterattack," he concluded, "we had to withdraw."[8]

Over the next few days, Stroop complained that, even as some of the resistance fighters were captured or killed, small bands of others would appear to take their place. He was particularly enraged by women guerrillas who called themselves *Chalutzim*. He described them as "firing pistols with both hands."[9] They also threw hand grenades that they had concealed in their underwear.

On the fifth day of the fighting, Stroop began to systematically burn down buildings. Many guerrillas were burned alive. Others jumped from burning buildings to the ground where they were shot and killed. Some guerrillas kept firing on the Nazis from the roofs of the burning buildings. Most of those who escaped fled into the Warsaw sewers.

Stroop tried to flood the sewers. The guerrillas battled their way to the control valves and stopped the flooding. The Germans dropped smoke bombs into the sewers through 183 manholes. That did not work either.

The scheduled three-day action lasted a month, until May 16. The Jews and Gypsies fought to the bitter end. Stroop reported the "total number of Jews dealt with: 56,065, including both Jews caught and Jews whose extermination can be proved." He put his own casualties at 16 killed and 90 wounded, but William L. Shirer, in his history of Nazi Germany, estimates that "the true figures were much higher."[10]

## Spontaneous Resistance

There was also resistance on the death trains. People pried off the floorboards and dropped to the tracks between the speeding train wheels. They tore the barbed wire from windows with their bare hands and jumped from the hurtling boxcars. Sometimes, unable to squeeze through themselves, they dropped their children out, yelling to them to run fast. When the children ran, the train guards fired on them with rifles and machine guns.

Often, those who escaped the boxcars were caught and shot by military patrols stationed along the tracks. Sometimes they were robbed and killed by local civilians. Only a few succeeded in escaping. This was unplanned resistance. So, too, were the early uprisings in the camps. They began in Belzec.

"The first one," according to a Polish underground report, "took place on June 13th [1942], when Jews were summoned to remove the corpses of murdered women and children." They attacked the guards, "which resulted in a struggle in which four to six Germans and nearly all the Jews died; several Jews managed to escape."[11]

On September 11, 1942, at Treblinka, a Jew named Meir Berliner took action on his own. Meir Berliner was an Argentinian citizen who had been visiting Warsaw with his wife and daughter when the Nazis seized them and sent them to Treblinka. His wife and daughter went straight to the gas chambers. Meir Berliner was assigned to a work detail.

In the evenings, the Nazi officer in charge, *Oberscharführer* Max Bialas, selected the weakest men and had them shot. One night Meir Berliner "jumped out of the ranks . . . with a drawn knife, and stabbed him in the back."[12] Meir Berliner was killed on the spot, and the next day 150 others were executed as punishment for the killing of Max Bialas.

## Organized Rebellions

One night in December 1942, two thousand Jews arrived at Treblinka. They were led in small groups to the gas chambers. Those remaining realized what was happening and "a great riot began."[13] A band of youths rushed the guards with knives and fists. Germans and Ukrainians fired into the crowd. A young Jew seized a grenade from a German soldier and hurled it, severely wounding a Ukrainian guard. Eventually the riot was brought under control, and the rioters were caught and killed.

Prior to this, escapes from Treblinka had been organized by Jewish and Gypsy prisoners and Russian POWs. Those left behind helped arrange the escapes and covered them up. When new shipments of prisoners arrived, individuals were hustled away from the lineups and sneaked into the general population where they answered to the escapees' names at roll calls.

Those who ran the camps tightened security with strengthened guard units, barbed wire, and land mines. Still the escape attempts continued. The most successful were by prisoners on work details outside the camps. In many instances, German and Ukrainian guards were killed with rakes and axes wielded by escaping slave laborers.

In 1943, undergrounds were organized in the concentration camps of Treblinka and Sobibor. On August 2, 1943, Treblinka prisoners attacked guards with hoes, pitchforks, and homemade knives. The rebellion continued, using guns and grenades captured from the guards. There were explosions, and fires broke out. While some fought the guards, 350 to 400 prisoners broke through the fence and escaped. Most were caught and killed. About 100 escaped and survived.

Poisonings were planned at Sobibor. Morphine was stolen from the infirmary. However, before the lethal doses could be administered to the guards the theft was discovered and the five people involved were taken out and shot.

There was a rebellion at Sobibor in October 1943. Some 300 prisoners escaped. About 150 were later caught and executed. A survivor described the uprising:

". . . Jews from Russia, Poland, Holland, France, Czechoslovakia, and Germany . . . pain-wracked, tormented people, surged forward . . . to life and freedom. . . ."[14]

There were similar uprisings in all of the camps in Western and Southern Europe as well as Eastern Europe. American, British, Russian, and other POWs risked death in a succession of escape attempts. Guerrilla fighters were active everywhere. In the most terrible circumstances, Jews, Gypsies, homosexuals, and various other Nazi-labeled *Untermenschen* all fought back.

They did not die without a struggle. They did "not go gentle into that good night," but rather went with "rage, rage against the dying of the light."[15] Such rage will always keep that light, the light of hope, alive.

# AFTERWORD

The Holocaust began with an idea. The idea is older than the Nazis. Centuries older. Thousands of years older.

It is the idea that one group of people is better than another group, that one race is better than another. One nationality is better than another. One religion is better than another.

Is there any truth to this idea?

Surely some of us are better than others in one way or another. Some of us are stronger, smarter, more nimble, faster, or healthier. We each vary from others in hundreds of ways that may be better . . . or only different.

Sometimes these differences even out. Sometimes they don't. People—individuals—are not the same.

We all fall short in one way or another. Sometimes we try to make up for it by finding ways in which our group is better. We take strength from the group; we find self-worth in it. We see our group as more moral, stronger, smarter, more honest, closer to God, superior in any one of a hundred different ways.

There is nothing wrong in taking pride in our race, our religion, or our country. The wrong creeps in when that feeling goes beyond pride. It begins with the belief that no matter how good or bad you are as a person you are superior because your group is superior to other groups. The danger is when you no longer take responsibility for your actions as an individual, but instead excuse them because they are part of a group action.

ONLY GUARD YOURSELF AND GUARD YOUR SOUL
CAREFULLY, LEST YOU FORGET THE THINGS YOUR
EYES SAW, AND LEST THESE THINGS DEPART
YOUR HEART ALL THE DAYS OF YOUR LIFE, AND YOU
SHALL MAKE THEM KNOWN TO YOUR CHILDREN,
AND TO YOUR CHILDREN'S CHILDREN.

The eternal flame in the Hall of Remembrance at the United States
Holocaust Memorial Museum in Washington, D.C.

Your merit as a person no longer has anything to do with how you behave, with how you treat others. Your group is superior, and therefore so are you. When this idea is embraced, there is terrible danger for all of us.

It contains the seeds of a holocaust in which we may all be swept up. Each of us is at risk. Each of us could end up a murderer.

Or a victim.

# CHRONOLOGY

| | |
|---|---|
| November 11, 1918 | Germany surrenders and World War I ends. |
| 1919–1920 | Weimar Republic is formed. |
| February 1920 | Nazis issue 25-point anti-Semitic party platform. |
| 1920–1923 | Nazis and Spartacists fight vicious battles in the streets. |
| 1923–1924 | Following the Beer Hall Putsch, Adolf Hitler writes *Mein Kampf* in prison. |
| 1929 | Geneva Convention Relating to the Treatment of Prisoners of War is passed. |
| January 30, 1933 | President von Hindenburg names Hitler chancellor of Germany. |
| March 1933 | First concentration camp opens at Dachau. |
| July 1933 | Nazis pass the Sterilization Law; Gypsies are specifically included as "lives not worthy of life." |
| June 1934 | The Night of the Long Knives; Hitler directs the murders of Nazi rivals and dissidents. |
| July 1934 | Nazis murder the chancellor of Austria. |
| August 1934 | Hitler combines offices of president and chancellor. |
| August 19, 1934 | 90 percent of German voters approve Hitler as dictator. |
| 1935 | Berlin police raid pubs frequented by homosexuals; homosexual magazines outlawed; Penal Code is amended to punish homosexuals. |
| September 15, 1935 | Anti-Semitic Nuremberg Laws are passed. |

| | |
|---|---|
| 1937 | Anti-Nazi minister Dr. Martin Niemöller is arrested. |
| 1937 | Roundups of Gypsies intensifies; they are herded into concentration camps. |
| March 12–13, 1938 | German army invades Austria and is welcomed. |
| April 10, 1938 | 99 percent of voters in both countries approve Germany's annexation of Austria. |
| October 5, 1938 | German troops occupy Sudetenland. |
| November 1938 | *Kristallnacht*: Jewish shops vandalized; synagogues destroyed. |
| Spring 1939 | Nazis institute Euthanasia Program authorizing killing of mentally and physically handicapped adults and children. |
| September 1, 1939 | Nazi troops invade Poland; World War II begins; mass roundups and killings of Jews and Gypsies begin. |
| 1939–1940 | Tens of thousands of Jews are herded into the Lublin District. |
| October 15, 1940 | Hitler decrees slave labor for Czechs and Poles. |
| June 22, 1941 | The German invasion of Russia begins. |
| July 1941 | Göring orders the "final solution of the Jewish question." |
| September 8, 1941 | The 872-day siege of Leningrad begins. |
| December 1941 | Hitler issues the Night and Fog Decree. |
| 1941–1942 | One million Jews are murdered, mostly by firing squads made up of SS troops, German Order Police, and non-German "helpers." |
| January 1942 | Göring orders life sentences for homosexuals; painful medical experiments on homosexuals begin. |
| | Wannsee Conference is held to arrange carrying out Final Solution more efficiently. |
| 1942–April 1945 | Operation Reinhard, the mass killing of millions of Jews in concentration camp gas chambers, is carried out. |
| June 1942 | The Lidice massacre takes place. |
| October 18, 1942 | Hitler issues top-secret Commando Order to kill prisoners of war in violation of the Geneva Convention. |

| | |
|---|---|
| November 14, 1942 | Forcible castration of homosexuals begins in concentration camps. |
| December 1942 | Newly arrived Treblinka prisoners riot against their guards. |
| 1943 | Treblinka and Sobibor camp inmates form underground organizations to plan, execute, and cover up escapes. |
| February 1943 | Nazis meet stiff resistance from Bialystok Jews. |
| April 19, 1943 | Germans launch "special action" against Warsaw ghetto and are driven back by organized Jewish resistance. |
| May 16, 1943 | After a month of bitter fighting and high Nazi casualties, the Warsaw ghetto resistance fighters are overcome. |
| August 1943 | Jewish women partisans battle the Nazis in Bialystok. |
| October 1943 | Sobibor prisoners rebel; 300 escape. |
| December 17, 1944 | The Malmédy Massacre takes place in Belgium. |
| April 1945 | Germany is defeated; Hitler kills himself; the war in Europe ends. |

# CHAPTER NOTES

## Chapter One

1. Justin Kaplan, ed., *Familiar Quotations, John Bartlett*, 16th ed. (Boston: Little, Brown and Company, 1992), p. 684.
2. *Encyclopaedia Britannica,* vol. 8 (Chicago: Encyclopaedia Britannica, Inc., 1984), p. 1185.
3. *Ibid.*, vol. IV, p. 466.
4. *Ibid.*, vol. 8, p. 1184.

## Chapter Two

1. Donald S. Detwiler, *Germany: A Short History*, rev. ed. (Carbondale: Southern Illinois University Press, 1989), p. 181.
2. J. Noakes and G. Pridham, eds., *Nazism: A History in Documents and Eyewitness Accounts, 1919–1945* (New York: Schocken Books, 1988), pp. 14–15.
3. Daniel John Goldhagen, *Hitler's Willing Executioners: Ordinary Germans and the Holocaust* (New York: Alfred A. Knopf, 1996), p. 84.
4. Alan Bullock, *Hitler and Stalin: Parallel Lives* (New York: Alfred A. Knopf, 1992), p. 418.
5. *Ibid.*, p. 145.
6. Goldhagen, p. 285.
7. Adolf Hitler and his associates, *Lunacy Becomes Us*, Clara Leiser, ed. (New York: Liveright Publishing Corporation, 1939), p. 93.
8. *Ibid.*
9. *Ibid.*
10. *Ibid.*, p. 42.

## Chapter Three

1. *Webster's New Universal Unabridged Dictionary* (New York: Dorset & Baber, 1983), p. 107.
2. Alan Bullock, *Hitler and Stalin: Parallel Lives* (New York: Alfred A. Knopf, 1992), p. 751.
3. Raul Hilberg, *Perpetrators Victims Bystanders: The Jewish Catastrophe 1933–1945* (New York: HarperCollins Publishers, 1992), p. 67.
4. William L. Shirer, *The Rise and Fall of the Third Reich: A History of Nazi Germany* (New York: Simon and Schuster, 1960), p. 235.
5. *Ibid.*
6. Günter Grau, *Hidden Holocaust*, trans. Patrick Camiller (New York: Cassell, 1995), p. 166.
7. Clifton Daniel, ed. *Chronicle of the 20th Century*, (Mount Kisco, NY: Chronicle Publications, 1987), p. 433.
8. Shirer, p. 233.
9. *Ibid.*
10. *Ibid.*, p. 239.
11. *Ibid.*
12. Daniel, p. 455.
13. *Ibid.*, p. 469.
14. Bullock, p. 567.
15. *Ibid.*
16. *Ibid.*, p. 568.
17. Peter Gay, *Freud: A Life for Our Time* (New York: W. W. Norton, 1988), p. 620.
18. Bullock, p. 656.

## Chapter Four

1. Max I. Dimont, *Jews, God and History* (New York: Signet, 1962), p. 17.
2. *Encyclopaedia Britannica,* vol. 8 (Chicago: Encyclopaedia Britannica, Inc., 1984), p. 253.
3. Ron Chernow, *The Warburgs: The 20th Century Odyssey of a Remarkable Jewish Family* (New York: Random House, 1993), p. 228.
4. *Ibid.*
5. *Ibid.*

## Chapter Five

1. Raul Hilberg, *Perpetrators Victims Bystanders: The Jewish Catastrophe 1933–1945* (New York: HarperCollins Publishers, 1992), pp. 148–149.
2. *Ibid.*, p. 301.
3. Yitzhak Arad, *Belzec, Sobibor, Treblinka: The Operation Reinhard Death Camps* (Bloomington: Indiana University Press, 1987), p. 14.
4. Daniel Jonah Goldhagen, *Hitler's Willing Executioners: Ordinary Germans and the Holocaust* (New York: Alfred A. Knopf, 1996), p. 149.
5. Arad, p. 7.
6. Christopher R. Browning, *Ordinary Men: Reserve Police Battalion 101 and the Final Solution in Poland* (New York: HarperCollins Publishers, 1992), p. 60.
7. *Ibid.*, p. 73.
8. Arad, p. 12.
9. William L. Shirer, *The Rise and Fall of the Third Reich: A History of Nazi Germany* (New York: Simon and Schuster, 1960), p. 965.
10. Arad, p. 64.
11. *Ibid.*, pp. 223–224.

## Chapter Six

1. William L. Shirer, *The Rise and Fall of the Third Reich: A History of Nazi Germany* (New York: Simon and Schuster, 1960), p. 937.
2. *Ibid.*, p. 938.
3. *Ibid.*
4. *Ibid.*, p. 939.
5. *Ibid.*, p. 854.
6. *Ibid.*, p. 938.
7. Joseph E. Persico, *Nuremberg: Infamy on Trial* (New York: Viking, 1994), p. 163.
8. Shirer, p. 947.
9. *Ibid.*
10. Harrison E. Salisbury, *The 900 Days: The Siege of Leningrad* (New York: Harper & Row, 1969), pp. 377–378.
11. *Ibid.*, p. 377.
12. Whitney R. Harris, *Tyranny on Trial: The Evidence at Nuremberg* (New York: Barnes & Noble Books, 1995), p. 185.

13. *Ibid.*, pp. 185–186.
14. *Ibid.*, p. 222.
15. Persico, p. 187.
16. Harris, p. 193.
17. *Ibid.*, p. 207.
18. *Ibid.*, p. 216.
19. Alan Bullock, *Hitler and Stalin: Parallel Lives* (New York: Alfred A. Knopf, 1992), p. 809.

## Chapter Seven

1. David Crowe and John Kolsti, eds., *The Gypsies of Eastern Europe* (Armonk, NY: M. E. Sharpe, Inc., 1992), p. 81.
2. Yitzhak Arad, *Belzec, Sobibor, Treblinka: The Operation Reinhard Death Camps* (Bloomington: Indiana University Press, 1987), p. 151.
3. Crowe and Kolsti, p. 14.
4. *Ibid.*, p. 15.
5. *Ibid.*, p. 16.
6. *Ibid.*, p. 17.
7. *Ibid.*, p. 18.
8. *Ibid.*, p. 43.
9. *Ibid.*, p. 154.
10. *Ibid.*, p. 41.
11. *Ibid.*, p. 45.
12. Justin Kaplan, ed., *Familiar Quotations, John Bartlett,* 16th ed. (Boston: Little, Brown and Company, 1992), p. 361.

## Chapter Eight

1. Günter Grau, *Hidden Holocaust,* trans. Patrick Camiller (New York: Cassell, 1995), p. 27.
2. *Ibid.*
3. *Ibid.*, p. 64.
4. *Ibid.*, p. 65.
5. *Ibid.*, p. 67.
6. *Ibid.*, p. 91.

7. *Ibid.*
8. *Ibid.*, p. 27.
9. *Ibid.*, p. 138.
10. *Ibid.*, pp. 11–12.
11. Stephan Likosky, ed., *Coming Out: An Anthology of International Gay and Lesbian Writings* (New York: Pantheon Books, 1992), p. 540.
12. *Ibid.*, p. 546.
13. *Ibid.*, p. 544.
14. Grau, p. 166.
15. *Ibid.*
16. *Ibid.*, p. 250.
17. *Ibid.*, p. 281.
18. *Ibid.*, p. 266.
19. *Ibid.*, p. 267.
20. *Ibid.*, p. 13.

## Chapter Nine

1. *Encyclopaedia Britannica,* vol. 4 (Chicago: Encyclopaedia Britannica Inc., 1984), p. 541.
2. *Ibid.*, vol. 4, p. 466.
3. Whitney R. Harris, *Tyranny on Trial: The Evidence at Nuremberg* (New York: Barnes & Noble Books, 1995), p. 226.
4. *Ibid.*, p. 227.
5. William L. Shirer, *The Rise and Fall of the Third Reich: A History of Nazi Germany* (New York: Simon and Schuster, 1960), p. 956.
6. *Ibid.*, p. 952
7. *Ibid.*, p. 954.
8. Harris, p. 182.
9. *Ibid.*, p. 182.
10. *Ibid.*, p. 183.
11. *Ibid.*, p. 243.
12. *Ibid.*, p. 180.
13. *Ibid.*, p. 441.
14. *Ibid.*, p. 181.
15. Shirer, p. 1100.
16. *Ibid.*, pp. 1114–1115.

## Chapter Ten

1. Lucy S. Dawidowicz, *The War Against the Jews: 1933–1945* (New York: Holt, Rinehart and Winston, 1975), p. 345.
2. Yitzhak Arad, *Belzec, Sobibor, Treblinka: The Operation Reinhard Death Camps* (Bloomington: Indiana University Press, 1987), p. 243.
3. *Ibid.*, p. 244.
4. *Ibid.*, p. 247.
5. Raul Hilberg, *Perpetrators Victims Bystanders: The Jewish Catastrophe 1933–1945* (New York: HarperCollins Publishers, 1992), p. 182.
6. William L. Shirer, *The Rise and Fall of the Third Reich: A History of Nazi Germany* (New York: Simon and Schuster, 1960), p. 975.
7. Hilberg, p. 184.
8. Shirer, p. 976.
9. *Ibid.*
10. *Ibid.*, p. 978.
11. Arad, p. 257.
12. *Ibid.*, p. 98.
13. *Ibid.*, p. 255.
14. *Ibid.*, p. 330.
15. Justin Kaplan, ed., *Familiar Quotations, John Bartlett*, 16th ed. (Boston: Little, Brown and Company, 1992), p. 737.

# GLOSSARY

Aryans — Indo-Iranian ancestors of Germans on whom Nazis based their master-race claims

Beer Hall Putsch — failed Nazi attempt to organize an overthrow of the Weimar Republic

Chancellor — the prime minister in charge of running the German government

concentration camp — place of confinement and slave labor for anti-Nazis and Jews

death camps — concentration camps equipped for mass killing

Diaspora — the scattering of the Jewish people over many lands

*Einsatzgruppen* — SS squads assigned to murdering Jews and others.

euthanasia — the killing of those who are hopelessly ill with or without their consent

final solution — the Nazi plan to kill off the entire Jewish population of Europe

gas vans — trucks with sealed compartments used to murder victims by carbon monoxide fumes

Geneva Convention — internationally agreed-upon rules covering conduct in wartime

genocide — the killing of a whole race, people, or nation

Gestapo — Nazi secret police active in rounding up Jews for the death camps

ghetto — originally, a sealed-off area where Jews were forced to live

guerrilla — volunteer member of a small group fighting the occupying Nazi army

Gypsies — dark-skinned, nomadic people of Aryan descent who were victims of Nazi genocide

Holocaust — systematic extermination of six million European Jews by the Nazis

*Judenrein* — free of Jews

lesbian — a woman attracted to other women

*Mein Kampf* (*My Struggle*)—Hitler's blend of autobiography and anti-Semitic call to arms

National Socialist German Workers Party — the Nazis

Operation Reinhard — Nazi plan for organized killing of Eastern European Jews and Gypsies

Order Police — reserve police units who helped round up and kill Eastern European Jews

partisan — anti-Nazi freedom fighter

pink triangle — the badge homosexual concentration camp prisoners were forced to wear

POW — prisoner of war

Romany — Gypsies

*Schutzmannschaft* — volunteers in Nazi-occupied countries who helped the SS slaughter Jews

slave laborers — Jewish, Polish, Czech, and other prisoners forced to work in German industry

Spartacists — militant left-wing street fighters in 1920s Germany

*Schutzstaffel* (SS) — Hitler's personal guard unit; expanded in the war to perform mass killings

sterilization — a medical procedure depriving a person of the ability to conceive a child synagogue — Jewish house of worship

*Untermenschen* — people that the Nazis labeled "less than human"

Wannsee Conference — 1942 meeting of Nazi leaders to plan how to kill Jews more efficiently

Weimar Republic — Germany between the fall of the kaiser and the rise of Hitler

Zionist — one who favors the establishment of a Jewish nation

Zyklon-B — the crystals from which the gas was made for mass killings in the death camps

# FOR MORE INFORMATION

Browning, Christopher R. *Ordinary Men: Reserve Police Battalion 101 and the Final Solution in Poland.* New York: HarperCollins Publishers, 1992.

Crowe, David, and Kolsti, John, eds., *The Gypsies of Eastern Europe.* Armonk, NY: M. E. Sharpe, Inc., 1992.

Dawidowicz, Lucy S. *The War Against the Jews 1933–1945.* New York: Holt, Rinehart and Winston, 1975.

Frank, Anne. *Anne Frank: The Diary of a Young Girl.* New York: Pocket Books, 1953.

Grau, Günter, ed. *Hidden Holocaust?* Trans. Patrick Camiller. New York: Cassell, 1995.

Handler, Andrew, and Meschel, Susan V. *Young People Speak: Surviving the Holocaust.* Danbury, CT: Franklin Watts, 1993.

Keneally, Thomas. *Schindler's List.* New York: Simon & Schuster, 1982.

Kuznetsov, Anatoly. *Babi Yar.* New York: Dell, 1967.

Landau, Elaine. *We Survived the Holocaust.* Danbury, CT: Franklin Watts, 1991.

Likosky, Stephan, ed. *Coming Out: An Anthology of International Gay and Lesbian Writings.* New York: Pantheon Books, 1992.

Lobel, Anita, *No Pretty Pictures: A Child of War.* New York: Greenwillow, 1998.

Opdyke, Irene Gut, and Jennifer Armstrong, *In My Hands: Memories of a Holocaust Rescuer.* New York: Random, 1998.

Persico, Joseph E. *Nuremberg: Infamy on Trial.* New York: Viking, 1994.

Rochman, Hazel, and Darlene Z. Campbell, eds. *Bearing Witness: Stories of the Holocaust.* New York: Orchard, 1995.

Shirer, William L. *The Rise and Fall of the Third Reich: A History of Nazi Germany.* New York: Simon & Schuster, 1960.

Yoran, Shalom. *The Defiant: A True Story.* New York: St. Martin's Press, 1996.

## Internet Sites

(All have links to related sites.)

The United States Holocaust Memorial Museum
www.ushmm.org

*The Holocaust: An Historical Summary*
www.ushmm.org/education/history.html

Holocaust Resources on the World Wide Web
www.fred.net/nhhs/html/hololink.htm

The Jewish Student Online Research Center (JSOURCE)
www.us-israel.org/jsource/

*Remembering the Holocaust*
yarra.vicnet.net.au/~aragorn/holocaus.htm

# INDEX

Page numbers in *italics* refer to illustrations.